Margaret Elise Harkness

Toilers in London

Inquiries concerning female labour in the metropolis. Being the second part of

Margaret Elise Harkness

Toilers in London
Inquiries concerning female labour in the metropolis. Being the second part of

ISBN/EAN: 9783337071875

Printed in Europe, USA, Canada, Australia, Japan

Cover: Foto ©Suzi / pixelio.de

More available books at **www.hansebooks.com**

TOILERS IN LONDON;

OR,

INQUIRIES CONCERNING FEMALE LABOUR IN THE METROPOLIS.

Being the Second Part of "Tempted London."

BY THE

"BRITISH WEEKLY" COMMISSIONERS.

Edited by the Author of "Out of Work," etc.

London:
HODDER AND STOUGHTON,
27, PATERNOSTER ROW.

MDCCCLXXXIX.
1889

"Is it well that while we range with Science, glorying in the Time,
City children soak and blacken soul and sense in city slime?
There among the gloomy alleys Progress halts on palsied feet,
Crime and hunger cast our maidens by the thousand on the street.
There the Master scrimps his haggard sempstress of her daily bread,
There a single sordid attic holds the living and the dead!"

CONTENTS.

CHAPTER I.

FLOWER-GIRLS.

THE flower-girl is such a familiar sight to Londoners, that few of us realise what the streets of the metropolis would miss if she were banished.

"The world would be a sorry place if it had no flowers in it," an old man said to one of our Commissioners, while he was buying some primroses from a girl at the corner of Oxford Street. It was Primrose Day, and the old man was fastening a small bunch of primroses in his coat when our Commissioner stopped beside the flower-girl's basket.

Fifteen years ago no flower-girls enlivened London thoroughfares. If people wanted flowers they were obliged to find a nursery garden, or to visit a market. At these places flowers were then very expensive; for the people had not at that time learnt to appreciate simple flowers like primroses and daffodils; they only cared for costly exotics.

Now any one can during the spring season buy enough flowers in the streets to deck a room for sixpence, and a small bunch of violets or a button-hole for one penny. Nothing comes amiss to the flower-girl's basket: snowdrops, crocuses, violets, "dim, but sweeter than the lids of Juno's eyes or Cytherea's breath;" "daisies pied, and lady-smocks all silver-white, or cuckoo buds of yellow hue, that paint the meadows with delight." These the flower-girl brings to us in the spring season. Later on she offers us roses and carnations, geraniums and mignonette. Last of all, she fills her basket with foreign flowers and ferns from the Continent. Every one buys of her; that is to say, every pedestrian, from the young girl, "a maiden in her flower," on her way to tennis, to the poor sempstress, whose home is a garret. Only the other day a working man, whose little child lay dead in a hospital, picked up a bunch of violets that some one richer than himself had bought from a flower-girl and thrown away, or dropped. He carried them to the mortuary, and placed them in the little dead child's cold fingers. As he left the place the nurse heard him say to himself, "The little 'un was always so fond of violets."

It is wonderful to witness the love which the poorest and lowest people in London have for flowers. They watch over their sickly geraniums and blighted dwarf rose-trees with more devotion than a gardener bestows on hot-house plants, which he expects to see later on carrying off prizes at exhibitions. In the East End markets, flowers in pots, musk plants, and shrubs, are sold to people who never eat meat during the week, who can scarcely afford to buy meat on Sunday. This love of flowers is one of the most hopeful symptoms in the condition of the *very poor* in London.

"I believe," says one who has studied the ways of such people closely, "that the bunch of violets, on which a poor woman or her husband has expended a penny, rarely ornaments an unswept hearth."

To learn how much the poor appreciate flowers, one has only to pass by our large London hospitals on a Sunday afternoon, at the hour when patients are allowed to see their friends and relations. Outside the hospital gates stand men and women selling flowers at low prices, flowers which are bought by poor people to give the patients. Also at the entrances of our great cemeteries flower-sellers take their stand on Sundays, and mourners purchase from them bunches of flowers to lay on the graves, or plants to place beside the tombstones of those who have gone over to "the great majority."

It is a fact that on Saturdays more flowers are sold in the London streets than on any other day of the week; and these are bought by working-men and working-women out of their small, hardly-earned wages.

Flowers carry a message of love and hope even to slum children. The following is a true anecdote.

When the present matron of the London Hospital was a nurse at the Westminster Hospital, a little child under her care became one night so ill that the house-doctor thought it was dying. This child had been brought from one of the slums that lie not far away from Westminster Abbey. It was accustomed to hear oaths, to see drunken quarrels; nothing else. When it lay near death, it was heard to say, "That's daddy," as a drunken man passed beneath the windows of the ward singing a ribald song accompanied by a volley of curses.

The nurse thought it sad that this child should pass away knowing nothing of earth but sin and misery. She had in her dress a bunch of violets which she had bought from a flower-girl's basket. She showed these violets to the child, who lay on her knee, and she spoke of a place called heaven, where all would be happiness, into which sorrow and sin would never enter. The child did not understand. So she took the flowers out of her dress, and said, "Look here, heaven is full of things like this; look at these violets!"

"Then I'll pick 'em, nurse," the child said, with that perfect faith which only comes to little children.

> "In all places then, and in all seasons,
> Flowers expand their light and soul-like wings,
> Teaching us by most persuasive reasons
> How akin they are to human things."

The *Pall Mall Gazette* gives the following description of a flower-girl's appearance:—

"Her gown is generally of dark stuff or print, practically short in the skirt, and over her jacket-bodice she wears a woollen shawl of bright, not to say gaudy hues, pinned across the bust to each side of her waist, whence depends an ample apron of unbleached linen or coloured print. Her black bonnet, if she wears a bonnet, will generally have a gay flower in it; a pair of bright metal earrings hang at her ears; her boots are strong and water-tight, laced with leather thongs."

This description is true with regard to all things but boots and bonnets. It would be well indeed if the flower-girl had strong and water-tight boots. The boots she wears are, as a rule, full of holes, and show her dirty stockings or naked feet. She generally buys her boots in old clothes-markets, and the sight of a good pair of boots on the feet of a flower-girl is so rare that our Commissioners assert it has never been their good fortune to witness it. The flower-girl seldom wears a bonnet. Her head-gear is almost always an old black hat, with a limp, coloured feather in front, and some bits of black ribbon or velvet at the back.

Even flower-girls belong to feather clubs. One girl collects the pence from the rest; then a raid is made on some shop where cheap coloured feathers are kept, in which ostrich tips can be had for twopence or threepence, and long ostrich feathers for one shilling or eighteenpence. Such clubs are to be found among working-girls all over London, and are rudimentary attempts at organisation which ought not to be scoffed at by those people who believe in the redemption of female labour by means of trades unions.

There are at the present time about 2,000 flower-girls in London. These figures include the girls who sell water-cress, and the girls who act as street-hawkers.

Flower-girls may be divided into two classes: those who sell by day and those who sell by night. It is needless to say which class is the most respectable. Sometimes girls of the first class are obliged to stay out until three o'clock in the morning, because they cannot get rid of their merchandise; but generally such girls go home at dark, and get up early in the morning to replenish their baskets. Girls of the second class come out at nine or ten o'clock at night and stay in the streets until the morning.

Flower-girls become street hawkers during the winter months, when flowers are scarce, and only the old hands can sell enough to keep body and soul together.

After "Lavender! sweet lavender! Who'll buy my sweet lavender?" has been heard in the suburbs, flower-girls fill their baskets with oranges, and go about singing, "Oranges, two-a-pinny oranges!" Or they sell dry goods, such as fusees and lucifer matches.

It is important to bear in mind that flower-girls and street-hawkers are the same individuals plying different trades at different seasons of the year. They sell flowers in summer, fruit and matches in winter. The water-cress seller belongs to their ranks. She is a poorer sister. The cress trade is chiefly carried on by old women, who buy it at one penny the "hand," and sell it outside factories and places of business. During mid-winter there is practically no water-cress; so the piteous tales which one reads about children shivering while they wash cress under pumps are rather exaggerated. Yet it is cold enough on February mornings; and one may then see barefooted children buying a "hand" or two "hands" of cress in Farringdon Market. These "hands" they sell again in back streets, and in mews, with a very small profit. Many a London child goes out thus to earn its breakfast. Its boots (if it has any) are kept at home, for otherwise it would not escape the School Board visitor whose business it is to hunt up truants.

A "hand" can be made by a clever cress-seller into four penny bunches. It is calculated that 15,000,000 "hands" of cress are sold in London during the year; but of course in a matter like this it is impossible to get accurate statistics.

A Commissioner reports the following case of a cress-girl, visited a few weeks ago at her lodging in Soho:—

"Mounting a steep, dark staircase," the Commissioner says, "I came to a room the door of which stood open. The room measured eight feet by ten feet, certainly not more. The window was broken, and a dirty yellow apron was stretched across the cracked glass. The furniture consisted of a four-post bedstead, on which were a filthy mattress and an old torn blanket. Underneath the bed stood a large basket, full of water-cress. Above the empty fireplace hung a rosary, and on the wall near the bed was a picture of the Virgin Mary.

"I lifted the yellow apron, and looked down into the yard. Dead cats, old baskets, bits of wood, rags and refuse, lay on the slanting roofs. Far down, almost further than I could see, stood a girl by a pump. She was filling a bucket, and I felt sure that she was the girl I had come to visit. So I waited. Presently she came upstairs, carrying the bucket. She did not inquire what I wanted, but began at once to wash her cress and to tie it up with rush. She took it as a matter of course that I had come to pay her a visit, and did not ask me 'to be seated,' as is the way in country cottages. She squatted on the floor herself, beside the bucket. She dipped the cress in water, and made it into bundles as though her fingers had been bits of machinery.

"After I had broken the ice by the gift of a soup ticket, she began to tell me her history. She was Irish. She lived in this room by herself, and paid for it 4*s*. 6*d*. per week. It was close to Covent Garden, so it was handy for the market.

"How much could she make in a day?

"That depended on the weather mostly. Sometimes she earned 1*s*. 6*d*., sometimes more, sometimes less. She was going to be married next week. She was tired of living by herself, and the 'chap' she meant to marry would carry her basket.

"What did he do?

"Oh, he did nothing. He sold flowers in pots sometimes, but mostly he did nothing.

"Did she go to church?

"Yes, to Mass once a year. She had a religion of her own, which was as good as any other religion. She worshipped the Mother of God. When she died she'd know 'the great secret.'

"What was that?

"If she'd a soul that would live again, or if she was nothing."

It is rare to find a girl selling flowers or water-cress in the streets who is not Irish and a Roman Catholic. Our Commissioners say that in nearly all the homes of such girls they have found pictures of the Virgin Mary and rosaries. It would seem that the Irish temperament lends itself to Bohemianism, and enjoys a roving life.

These girls believe in the Catholic religion to a certain extent. They do not believe much in anything. Their hand-to-mouth existence leaves them little time to think about religion, and their ragged clothes make them ashamed to enter churches.

They say: " A poor girl has other things to do than busy herself about religion. Religion's all very well for folks that haven't to earn their living, folks that have money and carriages. If a girl sells her flowers she's got enough to think about. Our Blessed Lady can't expect us to do more than say our beads of a Sunday, and go to Mass at Christmas."

Amongst these girls death is often called " the great secret." It is useless to pretend that they hold the doctrines of the Catholic Church with regard to heaven and hell. They sometimes say, " All must go to purgatory, you, me, and everybody."

But their faith does not stretch far into the future. Some are simple materialists, and very few trouble themselves about a life after death—in other words " the great secret."

The favourite haunt of flower-girls is Seven Dials. They live there in large numbers, also about Drury Lane and Soho. The neighbourhood suits them because it is near Covent Garden, at which place they must be early in the morning to buy flowers and green-stuff. Water-cress is sold at Covent Garden, also in Farringdon, Spitalfields, and the Borough markets.

But " Fresh wo-orter cree-ses ! " is becoming a rare cry in the fashionable parts of London. It is daily heard farther and farther away from the West End, in the East End, and in the outlying London districts.

Certainly if people could have a look at the rooms in which water-cress is kept after it leaves the market, if they could have a glance into the places which constitute " home " for poor water-cress sellers, they would never eat water-cress again, not even if they gathered it for themselves in country districts.

Imagine for a minute a running stream between two green meadows ! Look into the clear water, and see the water-cress moved backwards and forwards by the current ! Then picture it in a London market, after it leaves the hamper in which it has been tightly packed for twenty-four hours. See the grimy hands of the cress girl, and watch her carrying it home in her dirty apron. She takes it to a pump, and puts it into a bucket which is used for every imaginable domestic purpose. While she sweeps her room it lies under the bed, with nothing to cover it up.

So the filth of the place gives it a relish. Presently she turns it out on an old blanket, or upon the bed, and begins to tie it up with rush. Sometimes she nibbles a green leaf, or bites a stalk, while she arranges it in her basket. At last it is ready for customers. Then she puts on her hat, and carries it out in the street, crying, "Wo-orter cree-ses! *fresh* wo-orter cree-ses!" in a shrill voice.

This is the truth. It is far more romantic to think of the little cress-girl at the clean pump, although she may be shivering and have bare feet. As we said before, water-cress is "out of season" during the winter months, and is chiefly sold by old women.

Of course selling flowers is unskilled labour; yet few succeed in the business unless they are the daughters of street-hawkers, and have been trained to the work from infancy. To buy, to tie, and to sell are the three important lessons which a flower-girl has to learn. In order to buy well she must understand the market, she must know when to hold off, and when to step in and make her purchases. Some girls are so clever in their mode of buying, that they get their flowers and ferns for almost nothing. During the summer months Covent Garden is practically open all night, and quick girls know how to stock their baskets on market days with little money. They look out for leavings, and buy faded flowers for a mere song. The art of tying consists in wiring and gluing the flowers, in making the most of every leaf, in hiding faded goods behind fresh merchandise, and in arranging the flowers to advantage in the basket.

To sell well requires a certain knowledge of the human face and a pleasant address. It is a melancholy fact that flower-girls of the second class—namely, those who sell at night—make the greatest profits. Such girls are much patronised by a certain class of women, and can earn as much as £3 a week by selling flowers outside theatres and music-halls. Girls who sell by day make sometimes 10*s.* a week, generally less, and during wet weather little or nothing.

Flower-girls are an improvident race. They do not save money. Generally some old woman lends them what is called "stock-cash," and charges them an exorbitant interest upon it. They do not put by for a rainy day, unless they marry and become what they call "staid women." Most of them (as we said before) are Irish, and possess the facile tongue of their nation. Business is always "slack" with them; they never own to making money. But they have also the chief virtue of the Irish—they are exceedingly generous. They lend one another money and clothes; they buy for one another in the market; they share food and sleeping accommodation; they show one another an endless amount of kindness.

The highest ambition of a street-hawker is to possess a barrow and sell whelks. Twelve shillings is sufficient to start a whelk business. If a girl arrives at the possession of a barrow and the necessary paraphernalia of saucers, pepper-pot, etc., she can generally earn "a tidy bit of money." Women make such stalls look more attractive than men: they dish up the whelks with parsley, and scrub the saucers. Then they put on a clean apron, and with a pleasant smile beguile passers-by to indulge in a dainty dish which is much appreciated in some London districts.

But for one street-hawker who rises in life high enough to possess a whelk business, ten sink under the demoralising influence of street-life. Flower-girls deteriorate rapidly after they reach the age of fifteen. Everything that is "womanly" seems then to die out within them; they grow lawless, and lose all sense of what is "clean and decent." Many sink deep into the mire and are never heard of again, except in the lowest dens of the metropolis.

The *Pall Mall* calls them "girl graduates in

the school of vice." Certainly they tread a path that is beset with temptations. On wet days they take refuge in some public-house, and the post at which they can carry on the best business in winter is the entrance of a gin-palace.

Very few marry.

A Commissioner reports the following case, which gives an idea of what flower-girls call "being married."

She went to see a young couple who had started as husband and wife in a house near Drury Lane. They had hired an unfurnished apartment, for which they were to pay 3*s.* 6*d.* weekly. When she knocked at the door a voice said, "Come in." She found the bride and bridegroom at tea. They were sitting on the floor, drinking coffee out of the same white pot and eating slices of bread-and-butter. The room had not a vestige of furniture—nothing but four walls and a bare floor. There they sat, looking at one another, talking about the best way to buy next morning at Covent Garden Market. One shilling was all the worldly goods they possessed, so they were anxious to make the most of it. The bride was fifteen, and the bridegroom was about two years older. They looked very happy, and said that they supposed something would turn up next day in the way of money. Other folks had started like them, folks they knew well, not older than themselves, folks in the flower-business. The girl had no hat, only a print dress and a small shawl. The boy wore ragged clothes, and had no boots on his feet. They were not at all shy, and did not seem to think their conduct extraordinary. Needless to say, they had not been to church, so the girl would have no "lines" to show later on in case the lad "took up" with some other woman.

Directly a girl of this class leaves school she becomes eligible for the position of "round-the-corner" (sweetheart), and if her lad is willing to begin married life, she "gives notice" at home, and walks away with her "bits of things" to the room she is to share with him. Sometimes the acquaintance begins quite casually in a penny gaff.

After a few walks, the lad suggests that they may as well "put up together." He then treats his round-the-corner at the public-house, and they begin married life, careless of what people say, reckless of the future.

Only too often round-the-corners find their lads a sore burden, and bitterly regret the day on which they said "Yes" to a "lineless" marriage. But they are very faithful to their lazy husbands. It is an old saying:

"A dog, a woman, and a walnut tree,
The more you beat them the better they be."

Round-the-corners develop a slavish love for their lads, and not only work for them, but bear cuffs and kicks sooner than break away from "lineless" matrimony.

Our Commissioners report case after case in which the lad has been found in bed at twelve o'clock in the morning, while his round-the-corner has been busy selling flowers to provide him with breakfast. Lads like this begin with promises of carrying baskets, but soon sink into lives of complete laziness.

Few sights in London are prettier to witness than Covent Garden on Primrose Day, at half-past six or seven o'clock in the morning.

"That Bacon, what's his name, he's a good man," a Commissioner heard a flower-girl declare last Primrose Day. "I say, 'Long live Bacon, what's his name, and bless him for what he's done for us poor flower-women.'"

"Baconsfield! Why, he's dead and buried," said another girl. "Haven't you seen his monument, all done up with primroses, down opposite of Westminster Abbey? He's been dead and buried this long while."

"More's the pity," answered the first speaker. "He must have been a kind-hearted gentleman to think of us poor flower-women. It's a pity there aren't more of his sort. I'd like to have Primrose Day every week. It would suit my pocket."

Primroses and moss-roses are the flowers that sell best in the streets of the metropolis.

On Primrose Day not only the regular flower-sellers, but also cress-sellers, street-hawkers, and others buy primroses to carry all over London. Boys and girls thus make sixpence. Old men and women in this way take home a shilling. Lord Beaconsfield's name passes from mouth to mouth, and all agree that he was "a kind-hearted gentleman." Needless to say, these people do not trouble their heads much about politics. Their horizon is Covent Garden Market. A Commissioner was told the other day by a flower-seller in Cheapside that "Government" ought to look sharp there, and get the place fit for traffic. It was "mighty hard" on flower-sellers to be kept off their beat. "Government had no right to do it."

It is calculated that at least 3,000,000 flowers are sold in the London streets every year. Button-holes pay the best. Flower-sellers know how to keep these fresh; they manipulate them carefully, and handle them gingerly. So their "stock" lasts a week or a fortnight, and purchasers wonder why button-holes fall to pieces directly the fragile things come in contact with cold air or hot fingers.

Church festivals are a great boon to flower-sellers, also fashionable weddings, for which churches must be decorated. Large quantities of Lent-lilies and other cheap flowers find their way from the baskets of flower-sellers into the sacred buildings of the metropolis; and young ladies with High Church proclivities are looked upon as "good customers."

We have mentioned two classes of flower-girls: those who sell by night and those who sell by day. The latter class must be divided into button-hole sellers and sellers of flowers in bunches. The former frequent the City, Piccadilly, and Oxford Circus. The latter are to be found chiefly in Kensington, and in the fashionable parts of London. Gentlemen buy from button-hole sellers; ladies patronise the sellers of flowers in bunches. The latter consist in a large degree of young married women, and amongst these may be found many very respectable people.

The public is inclined to think flower-selling an open market. This is a mistake. There is barely room in it for the 2,000 girls and women who now try to earn their living by selling flowers and water-cress. Girls from factories, and young women whose fathers are out of employment, often imagine that they have only to buy a few flowers and sell them again in the streets in order to make a living. Such people find to their cost that even flower-selling needs an apprenticeship.

The following case, visited by a Commissioner, will give a very good idea of what the flower-market is like at present.

Mrs. —— has six daughters engaged in selling flowers about London. She lives in a street off Drury Lane; when our Commissioner called upon her at ten o'clock one morning she was preparing flowers for the baskets of her six daughters. She pays five shillings a week for two rooms and a small cupboard. The front room looks out on the street; the back room has no outlook. She is about forty-five, and a strong, stout woman, with what is called "a motherly presence."

She greeted our Commissioner pleasantly, and asked what flowers were wanted. While she was making up daffodils into bunches, she gave the following account of herself, and of her children.

"Yes, I've six daughters in the flower business. I was in it myself, so I brought 'em up to buy and sell sooner than see 'em go away from me. I buried my husband eighteen months ago. He was a good husband to me, and though he suffered a deal, he'd come down to the market and buy, never mind how ill he was, and he'd sell all day like me, never mind what he was feeling. One morning, eighteen months ago, I left him a-bed, and he said he'd be down at the market by seven o'clock. But he didn't come; and at eight my little girl, the youngest—that one there that's nursing my eldest daughter's baby—she came to me, and she said—

"'Mother, father went back to bed directly he'd had his breakfast, and he's lying so still. I can't wake him.'

"I went home, and I found him stone-dead. I fetched the doctor, and the doctor said he'd been dead an hour, most likely. My little girl, she'd never seen any one die, so she didn't know what it was. He must have gone off quiet."

Mrs. —— stopped to wipe her face with her apron, and went on to say—

"The doctor said his heart was weak, most likely. He never was a strong man, but he never used to complain of nothing."

Our Commissioner inquired how much Mrs. —— made in the week by selling flowers with the assistance of her six daughters.

"Depends on the market. If the flowers are good and cheap we get a tidy bit of money. If the weather's against us we do next to nothing. There's a many mouths to feed. My two eldest daughters are married. That's my eldest daughter's baby my little girl's nursing there by the fire."

"Who did they marry?"

"Labourers."

"So they leave their children with you, and still go out selling flowers in the streets?"

"Well, the eldest, her husband is out of work, and he can't mind the children because he's looking for something to do. He's a sober man, and he'd be glad of a job if you could recommend him. The other one, her husband don't earn much. I was glad to get 'em married. There's a many girls selling flowers what live with men without being married, so I'm not the one to stand against my daughters getting married, though they do put on me with their babies."

"You have been married more than once yourself?" remarked our Commissioner, looking at the large gold rings on her finger.

"Bless you! these rings is my stock money. When I save a goodish bit, I buy a gold ring, and if work gets slack I pawn it. I couldn't have money lying about, so I put it in a ring. Then it's no temptation to me nor nobody."

"I suppose you mean by 'temptation' the gin-shop?"

"Yes, that's it. I don't drink myself, but it's hard not to lend a few shillings if you have 'em, and then the folks drink and never pay you back. There's women now that owe me money, and I know I'll never see it again. It's the drink that ruins flower-women."

Afterwards Mrs. —— took our Commissioner to see her front room, of which she is very proud because of its "natty" appearance. Needless to say, she is a Roman Catholic.

The uncertainty of the life causes flower-selling to have a most demoralising influence on girls and women. If they are "flush," they find drink a great temptation. If times are bad, a glass of gin "raises their spirits," and helps them to "go on again." They are a short-lived race; for exposure to cold and damp ruins their constitutions. Also the gin they drink gives them a fictitious strength that vanishes at the approach of illness.

When ill they visit cheap dispensaries, where they can get advice and a bottle of physic for sixpence. A doctor's visit costs a shilling. They have a great dislike to hospitals, partly because they go in to be looked at with a herd of other patients, partly because of the off-hand manner in which they are received by young doctors who "practise" on out-patients.

"He spoke to me as if I were a dog," a Commissioner heard a flower-girl say as she left the out-patients' department of a large London hospital not long ago. "I'll die rather than demean myself to him. I won't go to that place again, not if I'm dying."

Even flower-girls do not like to be thought paupers. They prefer to pay sixpence or a shilling, if they can possibly manage it, rather than accept advice and medicine from hospitals and charitable agencies. They know only too well what it is to be "clamming;" their food is "sawney" and dry bread; but they have an independent spirit, which is fostered by an out-door life, and the constant hope that if things are bad to-day something will turn up to-morrow.

As we said before, they are exceedingly generous. Moreover, they often receive a shilling or half-a-crown if they lay their case before kind-hearted people who are accustomed to deal with them. Such people do not follow them to slumdom, so the condition of their homes remains unknown to the public. Occasionally a house in which they live gets "condemned," and then they wander on to another filthy den about which no one thinks of complaining.

On the whole, policemen are very good to them. They are not allowed by the law to stand still, and if an inspector of police comes by, his subordinates say "Move on, move on," to these flower-women. But at other times policemen give them a large license, unless they are very impertinent. They rarely get "run in," and if they do, it is because they *will* thrust their wares too near the faces of passers-by, who complain to policemen and threaten to prosecute them.

Their amusements are almost nil, if we except the public-house, where they "drop in" for gossip or a song "of an evening." It is no uncommon thing to see a girl of seventeen, with her husband and her baby, spending an evening in a gin palace. If the baby cries she gives it "a drop of something." Meanwhile she gossips with friends, and sips out of the pewter pot that stands on a form beside her. It is easy to say that she should not do this, but when one sees what her "home" is, one finds it difficult to mete out the harsh judgment that comes so readily to the lips of those who never venture inside the precincts of slumdom. Rents in London are exorbitant, and one room is all that such poor people can afford —a cold, draughty place in winter, a stifling den in summer. Close by is a gin-palace, lighted up to attract customers, full of the flower-girls' friends and acquaintances. Shining glasses and bright-coloured bottles ornament the shelves, and behind the bar stands a well-dressed publican, wearing a diamond ring, or a smartly dressed woman in silk and velvet. Songs are sung, music is provided gratis, so flower-girls forsake their small dingy rooms and flock into gin-palaces.

Occasionally two or three flower-sellers will drop in for a cup of tea at low coffee-houses, places in which the fare is much cheaper than at Lockhart's. Boys playing "shove a halfpenny," niggers performing strange antics, men having sham boxing-matches, enliven the scene; and the women collect a few farthings to pay for "a musical tea." The fun that goes on in such places is of the lowest possible description, and the language we cannot tell to "decent, happy folks."

Many flower-sellers speak a jargon which is only understood by themselves. They pronounce words backwards, and abbreviate sentences.

Some well-meaning ladies opened a club for girls of this sort not far from Seven Dials. They were obliged to close it, for they could not understand a word the girls were saying. Other clubs for these girls have been more successful, but all such places need a great deal of tact and patience.

Sometimes during the summer flower-sellers take a ticket to Brighton, and sell flowers during the journey. They return late at night, after spending a few hours by the sea and many hours in the train. In the hop season they go to Kent, and thus earn what they call "back money," namely, back rent. Four or five pounds is considered "a tidy bit of money" to make by picking hops; for the journey is expensive, and wet weather frequently makes work slack. The accommodation provided for hop-pickers varies very much. Sometimes they occupy comfortable little cottages; sometimes they sleep in tents. It is no uncommon thing to see these poor women lying on wet straw, without any other covering than a bit of sacking or an old blanket. Many a flower-seller "gets her death" by picking hops; and most say "it isn't worth the trouble and the money."

"Our Lord Shaftesbury," as flower-sellers call the grandfather of the present Earl, was very kind to all engaged in selling flowers and water-cress. In his time flower-girls certainly had good boots, and those must have been the boots which the *Pall Mall* speaks about in the article we have already quoted.

Every one has heard about the donkey which the costermongers presented to Lord Shaftesbury. It was sent to St. Giles's, and there "waxed fat and kicked." The present Earl had many a ride on "Coster" when he was a little boy, and visitors at St. Giles's were always taken to see the costermongers' donkey.

But the clock which the flower-sellers gave to Lord Shaftesbury in recognition of his kindness has seldom been heard about. The old lady at the Bank who presented it still talks of the day, and says her legs shook so much that she nearly let it fall, "which would have been a pity, as it was real marble, and worth a sight of money."

The Emily Loan Fund, which Lord Shaftesbury instituted for the benefit of flower-sellers, is of inestimable service. From this fund money for stock is provided, and to the honour of the people who use it, we can say *on good authority* that the borrowed money is most faithfully given back again. The loans are issued upon the security of a respectable householder, and are repaid free of interest. About 300 loans are made every year from this fund, and many a flower-seller has to thank Lord Shaftesbury for the roof above her head, and the "stock" which helped her to keep out of the workhouse.

The loan forms a branch of the Water-cress and Flower-girls' Mission in Clerkenwell. It is a far cry from the West End to this place, and very few people pay a visit. Yet once upon a time "quality" lived there.

Margaret, Duchess of Newcastle, who was maid of honour to Henrietta Maria, who fled with her to France, and who at the Restoration returned to England, lived in Clerkenwell, where she wrote poems, plays, and philosophical works, such as "Observations upon Experimental Philosophy." Her monument is in Westminster Abbey, but people seldom think of her. She kept a large number of young ladies to write as she dictated, and used to call them up at all hours of the night when a new idea came to her.

Close to the place in which this famous lady lived and wrote is the Flower-sellers' Mission House, where girls of tender age, who have been persuaded to give up street life, are taught to make artificial flowers, and prepared for situations. There is no word so repugnant to a flower-girl as "service."

"I'll go to prison sooner than be a servant," such a one says when asked if she will enter the Mission. With her the word is synonomous with drudgery, loss of freedom, and oppression; and little wonder, considering what the life of a "slavey" is in most houses. But flower-girls take kindly to the work of making artificial flowers. The labour is light. It only requires deft fingers and the taste which such girls must possess in order to display flowers well in their baskets.

Artificial roses are made of cambric and muslin. Placing a leaf on a block of wood, the girl heats a metal ball at a gas stove, and by means of the handle presses the ball on the leaf, causing the latter to bulge out in the centre. Then, with the assistance of a small pair of delicate pincers, the leaf is "crimped" at the edges, and rolled up to form the inside of the rose. The leaves are attached to a gutta-percha stem with needle and thread. Flour-paste is used for the larger rose leaves and the green leaves. A small bead is slipped up the stem to keep the structure steady, and afterwards the rose is dried and finished.

The Flower-girls' Brigade had a stall at the Manchester Exhibition, which attracted a good deal of notice.

Many girls have passed through the hands of this Society, and in a quiet way it makes itself felt everywhere among flower-sellers, although the greater number of them are Roman Catholics, people who "do not hold" with the Protestant religion.

No one has, perhaps, a better knowledge of these women than Mr. Lynes, the missionary who for years has laboured amongst them night and day, who has ruined his health in the work, and who even now goes from beat to beat, speaking a kind word or taking a tired woman into a shop for a cup of tea. He enters into all their difficulties, and understands the hardships which they have to endure in their nomadic existence.

He can tell tales of humble heroism which will "give thoughts that do often lie too deep for tears," and point out *why* flower-sellers become only too often the victims of brutal, hulking fellows who live on them. They begin "lineless" marriages very young, before they are old enough to know what will happen, and when they wish to break away they find themselves tied by invisible strings to the fathers of their offspring.

Now we must leave flower-sellers and pass on to those girls who are engaged in home-industries. Flower-sellers breathe the sweet air of heaven, and handle nature's fairest products. These girls pass their lives in sunless rooms, and seldom see a flower unless it blooms in some East End market.

CHAPTER II.

MATCH-BOX MAKERS.

MATCH-BOX making is one of the standard supplementary industries of women who work at home in East End districts.

The worker fetches the materials, *i.e.*, thin wood shavings and papers, supplies the labour, paste, and hemp (the latter is used to tie the boxes up in bundles), and carries back the completed boxes. Every box consists, as we all know, of two parts, the case and the tray. Each box must pass eight times through the maker's hands. The tray, or drawer, consists of a strip of wood, notched for the four corners. This has to be bent into form ; if it is bent on the wrong side the wood snaps, and is spoiled. Then a strip of thin coloured paper (which has already been pasted) is folded round it, leaving a deeper margin at the bottom than the top. The upper edge is folded down over the upper rim, the lower edge is flattened out to support the bottom of the drawer, and the bottom is then neatly dropped in, and pressed flat upon the pasted paper. Thus there are four operations: (1) the bending and papering; (2) the folding of the upper edge; (3) the folding of the lower edge; (4) the putting in of the bottom. That is for the tray.

Now for the case. This, like the tray, has to be bent up and held together by the pasted paper. But the larger surface of paper demands a second operation of smoothing. Finally, a strip of sand-paper has to be fixed on the side, the pressing on of which makes unaccustomed fingers sore. There are thus three operations for the case. The eighth, and final process, is the fitting together of case and drawer, which must not be done until both are dry. After this the boxes have to be tied up in packets of one or two dozen.

Just now there seems to be a run on magenta match-boxes. There is quite a peculiar glow of colour in the bare uncarpeted room of a match-box maker, strewn as it is with these brightly-coloured little objects.

The most successful match-box maker our Commissioners have seen is a young unmarried woman, who lives alone in a back room, in a dull little street in Bow. She is an independent girl, who is not inclined, as she says, "to work under anybody." Her room, though bare, is bright and above the average as to cleanliness. The deal table stands under the window, and on it are arranged her papers, strips of wood, and paste. Her floor is pink with boxes. Of course a fire burns in her grate, for the match-boxes must be dried one way or another. If they are taken back damp she is obliged to carry them all home again. In fine weather they will dry in the air, but if the sun is too hot they curl up and warp. Then they remain upon the maker's hands, useless. Miss O—— presents quite a pleasant picture as she sits plying her deft handicraft by the clean deal table. Her dark hair might be better brushed, perhaps; her brass earrings are rather too long for the taste of the fastidious, and her working dress is a little shabby. But there is nothing abject or down-trodden about her. She is one of the few who have deliberately followed match-box making as a trade to live by. She has worked at it from childhood; so have all her sisters until they married. She fetches her work from a well-known great factory.

"Do they ever keep you waiting?" inquired our Commissioner.

"They don't keep *me* waiting," replied Miss O——, rather loftily.

All the time she was talking her hands were

busy with little strips of magenta bordering, over which she passed her paste with great rapidity.

"How many gross can you make in a day?" asked our Commissioner.

"By getting up at five, and working till nine in the evening, I can do eight gross."

"Does that include the time spent in fetching and carrying?"

"Yes."

"Do you always get up at five o'clock?"

"Yes."

Miss O—— is not loquacious.

She receives, of course, 2¼*d.* per gross; and we must subtract, say, 1*d.* a day for flour to make paste, and 1½*d.* per day for hemp to tie up the parcels. That is to say, she earns 1*s.* 6*d.* per day, less 2½*d.* Thus by working thirteen hours a day she makes 1*s.* 3*d.* Miss O—— is fortunate enough to have a constant supply of work, and not to be kept waiting for it; but she is exceptional in these points, as well as in her skill.

"I was told," said our Commissioner, "that the girls on view at the People's Palace some time since made twelve gross a day, and that the public was convinced match-box making was not ill-paid after all."

"I daresay they might," said Miss O——; "they had all their things laid ready for 'em, and had not to stop to pick 'em up, or put 'em to dry, or fit 'em together, or fetch 'em and carry 'em back again. They asked me to be one of 'em at the People's Palace, but I was ill and I couldn't go."

This little statement led our Commissioner to think that Miss O—— is a quick "hand," and also furnished an instructive commentary upon the value of the exhibition, which appeased the public conscience. On the other hand, it shows that the price of 9*d.* per day, recently given as the earnings of a match-box maker, is certainly not the highest reached. The average match-box maker—when she can get the work—who works steadily during the greater part of the day, would seldom fall below six gross a day, which gives 1*s.* net earnings. Putting the working hours at twelve (a low estimate), this gives a wage of precisely 1*d.* per hour.

Miss O—— has preferences for some kinds of match-boxes. She does not like to do the smaller ones, which, on the other hand, some workers prefer. She is in the fortunate position of being able to have what she chooses. Most women must take what they can get.

A daughter-in-law and mother-in-law, who work together in Bethnal Green, have a different fancy.

"I can't make the case," says the daughter-in-law, "and my mother-in-law, she can't make the tray."

This mother-in-law is an Irish woman, who worked in a lead factory until lead poisoning compelled her to give it up. Before going to the lead factory she had been a regular hand at match-box making, and declares that she could then make her ten gross a day. This statement is, however, probably due to her Hibernian imagination; for it is certain that she cannot make anything near ten gross at present. These two women live in the Old Nichol Street district of Bethnal Green. This small area lies close to Shoreditch Church, and was once the seat of the French silk-weaving trade. Some of the names, such as Turville, Fournier, and Chambord Streets, still speak of a French origin, and many of the houses have long windows in their upper storeys, under which the weavers wrought at their looms. Some trace of French descent still lingers—or so we fancy—about the faces and the manners of the people in Old Nichol Street district. The neighbourhood has a bad name, and is said to be the resort of thieves, but our Commissioners report that the people seem to be engaged in honest industries. The houses are poor and in ill repair, and the observant will see reason to suspect a general absence of dust-bins and other sanitary conveniences. But with all their faults the houses have some good old work in them, and the large weavers' windows let in light and air. Unfortunately, the inhabitants do not appreciate these blessings; as a rule, they seem to relish a stuffy atmosphere. The window of one house visited by our Commissioner stood open, and close by were two flower-pots. The one contained a rhubarb plant, the other a crop of parsley. On the window-sill were rows of pink boxes drying. There was no fire in the grate. Our Commissioner congratulated the woman on the good drying weather, but the woman shook her head, saying that she had no money to buy coals to dry the match-boxes. At the bottom of the staircase was a baby, just able to walk. The mother looked ill-fed, but the baby was fat and rosy, its golden hair was brushed, and its little scarlet pinafore was whole. It was too young to be at work with its mother; but children of three or four are often seen at work match-box making.

A Commissioner has been shown a little girl in a Board School who at six years of age could make four gross a day, and whose dexterity in this way is the constant temptation to her mother, who also makes match-boxes.

The girls who work at home are not very many in number; and they are generally the daughters of careful mothers who prefer to keep their children at home, or else independent-minded young women who, like Miss O——, do not find marriage *per se* an attraction. The latter are girls of some individuality and considerable self-reliance. They are, on the whole, a little more "stand-off-ish" than their married sisters, and have to be won by degrees to give information. Theirs is rather the tone, "Oh yes; I can show you if you like;" while the married woman shows a more sociable, not to say gossiping, disposition. The single woman of this type is apt to explain that "she keeps herself to herself," and does not care to know other people's business.

Miss O—— explained that such was her case; but her plan of "keeping to herself" did not exclude a little girl belonging to the house. This child stole in with a shy smile at the stranger, picked her way among the boxes on the floor, and sat herself down on the floor, taking for her seat a bundle of firewood.

"Lottie mostly comes and sits with me," said Miss O——, looking at the child with a kind smile, "and she's as quiet and good as possible."

The child was evidently quite at home, and quite happy in the room full of match-boxes.

Another match-box maker, a young woman

with several children, who lives near Miss O——, supports herself and family by this trade. Work is slack with her. She is not such a hand as Miss O——, and three gross a day are all she has made lately. The eldest girl, now over school-age, helps her.

The trade of match-box making was not always so ill-paid as at present. An old woman in Bethnal Green, who claims to have been working in the trade from its beginning, speaks of a golden age in which 4*d.* per gross was paid. One of the firm of Bryant and May, however, denies that that firm ever paid so much; $3\frac{1}{2}$*d.* is a price named by several women as formerly paid. Competition among the workers, and monopoly among the makers, have brought about the reduction.

A rumour is current in Bow that the boxes are now beginning to be made by machinery, and the work is said to be slack on this account. Metal match-boxes, of course, are, and have long been, made by machinery; but the introduction of machine-made wooden boxes—if it has indeed taken place—can only be very recent.

The whole industry, however, of match-making, with the vast percentages of the share-holders and the scanty pittances of the box makers, will probably be extinguished during the next ten years by the development of electric lighting. In the meantime foreign competition presses hard. The box makers of Bethnal Green complain sadly that work is slack "because of them Swedish matches."

"I daresay you don't know what they are," said one woman to a Commissioner. "These are what's ruining us."

And she took down *from her own mantelshelf* a box of the foreign matches!

Closely allied to match-box making is fancy-box making—namely, the forming of boxes for boots, collars, ties, corsets, buttons, bonnets, etc.

This occupation is pursued both in homes and factories. The rate of payment varies considerably.

Some women can earn comfortable wages by reasonable hours of work; some say justly that they think the match-box making is not quite so bad as their trade.

A Commissioner visited a woman lodging in Bethnal Green. There was a little shop on the ground-floor containing one sack of something. The landlord had up a notice that he mended boots; but he was sitting unoccupied in his dark shop, with a gloomy smile on his face. He was very old, very grimy, and very ill-tempered. Being asked for Mrs. Goodluck, he broke out—

"Good luck! Not much good luck she brought him. She owed him her rent, and out she would have to go. He was not going to keep her. Goodluck, indeed!"

The Commissioner went up a filthy staircase. Two scared, dirty little children, inheritors of the cruelly ironical name, replied, when they could be made to understand who was wanted, "mother was out."

They did not seem to know their mother's name or their own, whither she had gone, or when she would return. That they were Mrs. Goodluck's children was only learned from a young woman on the other side of the landing. This young woman opened her door very cautiously, and looked out with the scared eyes of a hunted animal. She was perhaps twenty-three, very thin, and very dirty. Her room, as seen from the doorway, looked literally and absolutely bare. There was nothing visible in it but dozens of bright green boxes—such boxes as buttons or collars might be packed in—and the materials for making more. These boxes have to be made and covered, and the lids have to be made and covered. The worker finds paste or glue (generally glue), and hemp for tying up the completed work. The price paid for these boxes is 3½*d.* per gross. She did not seem to know how many she could make in a day, but the testimony of a woman who makes such boxes seems to point to three gross being the outside number it is possible to make daily. The entire covering both of box and lid with stiff paper, necessitating the covering of the whole surface of cardboard with paste or glue, takes a long time. In fact, this work is, in the most literal sense, paid at a starvation rate. The woman was afraid to open her door on account of the landlord; she clearly lacked food, she had apparently no change of clothing, and was without any of the ordinary necessaries of life. Her room was filthy in the extreme. But how can a woman too poor to possess brush, broom, or pail clean her room? How can she even wash her face or hands? Our Commissioner says that she will never be able to look at a bright green square box in a draper's shop without recalling that woman's face, and the frightened eyes fixed on the staircase up which the landlord would come later on to demand the rent of her dirty apartment.

A woman who makes boot boxes, and who also lives in Bethnal Green, was visited afterwards. Her work is done in a kitchen. Everything there is of the same hue—one grimy grey —wood, walls, floor (the last a shade blacker), dress, even the hair of the worker. Piles of scored millboard and strips of paper—blue, orange, white, and green—lie in a corner, and a pot of glue stands on the table.

"What do you get for them?" inquired our Commissioner.

"One and ninepence a gross, and I have to find the glue and the hemp for tying 'em up, you know. And it takes a lot of glue, too, for these big boxes. I reckon a pound to the gross. You can't get it for less than 5*d.* and the hemp's ¾*d.* a ball, and it takes two to tie up a gross—that's 1½*d.* for hemp."

"So, taking it altogether, you get 1*s.* 2½*d.* a gross. How many can you make in a day?"

"Well, not a gross, do what I will; and I can't take in a whole gross at once, they are so big. It's cruel, that's what it is! It's worse than the match-box making."

Our Commissioners say that they experienced great difficulty in finding the homes of these poor box-makers. In the neighbourhoods in which such people live few doors retain any numbers. A scrawl of chalk is all in most cases. The non-existence of numbers does not, however, seem to be felt as an inconvenience by the inhabitants.

"The next house but one to the public-house

on the other side of the way," is the sort of direction given in these districts.

One fancy-box maker was found in a street that has quite a different aspect. This lies a little to the east of the old Nichol Street district. Here doorsteps are white, windows are clean, birdcages hang on the walls. Mrs. W—— inhabits a clean room, and shows her work readily. She is quite young, and wears the deep fringe and exaggerated dress-improver of the factory girl; but she is neat, not to say smart in appearance. She makes the square bonnet-boxes covered with bronze paper used by milliners. Before her marriage she worked in a City factory, where she made boxes for ties, "block-work"—that is to say, boxes fitted with a block on each side, and having a space between for the ties. She gets 6*d.* a dozen for her bronze paper boxes, which is good money.

Box-making is well paid in most of the large factories; but all about the East End women are to be found making boxes in their own homes at a starvation rate of payment.

CHAPTER III.

PALM-WORKERS.

OUR Commissioners give a deplorable account of the poverty and distress which they have witnessed during their inquiry into home industries. House after house, street after street, has shown men out of work, wives and daughters supporting the whole family.

They say that they wish readers could accompany them in their visits to the homes of the girls and women they have been obliged to see lately. The hardest part of their work consists of visits paid to starving people. The women flock out of their houses when they hear that an inquiry is being made into home industries and mob our Commissioners to ask, "Have you got work for us?" Girls run after them down the streets, and men follow them to the railway-station. They have not once been asked for money, only for work; and all they can do is to show their empty pockets.

A Commissioner reports a poor woman visited near Shoreditch, whose husband is out of work, and who has not had work herself lately. She weaves fringes for toilet-covers, and is paid two shillings for a piece thirty-six yards in length. Her husband puts the cotton on the loom for her over-night, and if she gets up at 4 a.m. and works until 11 p.m., she can make a piece in one day. But lately she has not had any work. When our Commissioner went into her room it presented a strange picture of cleanliness. The floor was white, and the furniture had not a speck of dust upon it. A clean patchwork-quilt covered the bed, and the empty grate was spotless. By the table stood two little children, without shoes or stockings, but as clean as the furniture; and the mother was clean herself, although her apron consisted of an old sack, and she wore a piece of sacking over her shoulders. The poor thing burst out crying when our Commissioner spoke about the fringe for toilet-covers, and said that she had had no work lately. No food had touched her lips that day, and the children had been to school without any breakfast.

People often say, "If things were really as bad as this we should hear more about it." Only those who go amongst the London poor can interpret their silence. They are still because they are starving. Nothing saps a man's strength like being hungry. Hunger takes all the spirit out of the unemployed, and so the public are inclined to think " Outcast London " a myth, and " Bitter cries " sensational stories. An intelligent working-man said to one of our Commissioners, " If we broke the heads of fifty Jews down here in Whitechapel something would be done to prevent this immigration. While we content ourselves with singing ' England for the English,' Government will say that these foreigners are a blessing to us."

It would be impossible to notice all the home industries, for their name is legion. Thus a little colony of women near Hackney are engaged in mending bad nutmegs. They fetch the worm-eaten nutmegs from factories, and mend them with nutmeg dust. A good nutmeg is ground very fine, and the dust is mixed with glue or gum. The mixture is then used to fill in the holes, and the mended nutmegs are returned to the manufactory. They are paid by the gross; but our Commissioner could not find out how much the women receive for their work. The women visited by our Commissioners are sometimes afraid of being " told upon ; " and although they are generally willing to give any amount of information about the work of their neighbours, they often keep a discreet silence with regard to their own particular industry. But owing to the fact that most of the workers possess the same failing, it is not difficult to arrive at a general idea of what the pay is all round in most of the home industries. So far as our Commissioners could gather, the gum and the good nutmegs are supplied to mend the worm-eaten wares, and twopence per gross is paid for the mended nutmegs.

Another small industry is that of making necklaces for China and Japan. This is practised in several parts of the Tower Hamlets. Beads and clasps are supplied; but the workers must provide the cotton on which the beads are strung. The usual pay for these necklaces is 2*s.* 3*d.* per gross, and a worker can make half a gross in the day, if she "sits at it." These necklaces consist of four rows of beads, twisted, and fastened with a metal clasp. They are made up into packets of a dozen, or half-a-dozen, and are returned to the manufactories. Fetching and taking back form an important part of the work, as the manufactories often lie far away from the homes of the workers. A Commissioner visited two girls who earn their living by stringing beads, and found them busy at work. Both girls were dirty, untidy, and badly fed. They gave a sad account of their life when "slack" times prevent them from having enough to eat and drink. The room they live in is small, and at the top of a lodging-house. They pay for it 3*s.* 6*d.* per week, and are in arrears for rent. It is a "furnished" apartment, and the furniture consists of a bedstead, a table, and two chairs. "The boxes are ours," they said. "But there's not much in 'em, for we've pawned all our clothes, mostly." The bed was covered with old newspapers, and on these were strewn white china beads in large quantities. One girl stood up stringing the beads, the other sat by the table fastening the clasps to the ready-made necklaces. A tin teapot was on the hob, and some slices of bread-and-butter were ready for "dinner." When asked if their usual fare consisted of tea and bread-and-butter, they answered "Yes."

"Do you ever get meat?"

"Well," said the eldest, who looked delicate, "I just *longs* for it."

These girls make a variety of cheap necklaces, but their chief work consists in stringing coloured beads for "foreign parts."

"I've seen necklaces like those we make in a shop near Bishopsgate," one girl said. "I don't think English girls wear them, but perhaps they are sold to the Jewesses."

In the neighbourhood of Holborn a great deal of work is done by girls and women for the fashionable shops, especially the re-lining of fur muffs and jackets. A Commissioner visited a poor woman near Red Lion Square the other day who had been out of work for some time, but who had just received an order from a well-known shop. When our Commissioner called, the woman was discovered sweeping the floor of her dirty little room, and emptying the contents of her dust-pan into a basket.

"What are you going to do with that dust?" our Commissioner asked.

"Well, you see, I'm short of wadding," the woman said. "They won't pay me till I take the work back, and I've not got any more wadding. If I go to the shop they'll say I was careless, so I'm just filling in with these sweepings."

On the table lay a magnificent seal-skin jacket, which had been sent by its owner to the shop for repair. Little does the owner of that jacket think that she will wear next winter the sweepings of a filthy little den in the neighbourhood of Red Lion Square!

So far as we are aware, no one has yet written "the history of a palm-thimble;" but when this is done, it will be so pathetic that readers will say, "It is not a true story." Directly a thing is told that pricks the conscience of the reader, we hear, "You are sensational," and when against the will tears come to the eyes of readers, they tell us, "It is not a true story."

A palm-thimble can be bought for *2s. 6d.* This is made of lead. Steel palm-thimbles are very expensive. But the latter wear a long time; and it is the ambition of every palm-worker to possess one. Those made of lead wear out very fast, and the needle is apt to slip off them into the hand of the worker. Palm needlewomen have shown their right hands to our Commissioners, scarred with wounds made by the needles that have slipped off the lead and gone deeply into their flesh. Such wounds take a long time to heal, and prevent women from working. The lead or steel is rather larger than the top of an ordinary thimble, flat, round, and placed in the centre of a broad piece of leather. This leather is fastened with a buckle and strap round the palm of the worker's hand, so that the piece of steel or lead comes exactly in the middle of the palm, and the needle can be pressed with all the manual force of which the worker is possessed into the canvas.

A Commissioner reports a palm-worker visited in Aldgate, a widow with two children. The eldest girl helps her mother, and some of the work is done by the grandmother. The three work in the same small room; one stands by the bed, the second stands by the table, the third stands by the fireplace. Palm-workers do all their work standing up; sitting down they would not have enough force to pass the long needles through the stiff canvas. These three women do "Government work." They think that the Government is responsible for their hardships, and speak as if Government were a Pharaoh in Egypt.

"I suffers murder from pins and needles in my hands at night, all along of Government," says the mother.

"The work tears my clothes to bits; I wish Government had to pay for them," says the daughter.

"Men used to get *7s.* for ten sacks, and Government only gives *4s.* for ten to us poor women," says the grandmother.

At the present time they are making coal sacks for ships. Each sack has four splices, eight holes, two patches. Each sack is sewn and roped. Each sack has a broad R worked on it for Government.

By working hard the mother can make such a sack in two hours; and she receives 4¾*d.* for it.

How hard the work is our readers can guess when they hear that she has sprained both of her wrists over Government work. Yet her only complaint is, "I can't get enough of it." She says, "Such a lot flies to the work that it's eaten up quick, and if Government liked it could get the work done for next to nothing. I work from five in the morning till late at night, and I'd work all night long if I could get more to do. I want to bring my girl up to something better than Government work. But work's difficult to get anywhere, and she set herself against going into service."

"They *do* say about here as the men will have to stay at home and mind the children, because the women are getting the work," said the grandmother. "She was a wicked woman who made the first sack for Government. Government was obliged to pay the men, but it can get women for next to nothing."

Another woman, visited in the far East, works for a well-known manufacturer. She makes tarpaulins for barges, break covers, blinds for shops, tents, sacks, etc. When our Commissioner called, she was sitting at her door. "School Board" (the School Board visitor) "told me you were coming," she said. "I thought maybe you wanted a charwoman."

"Then you are slack just now?"

"Yes, nothing's going on in our trade; it's all getting done by machinery; there'll be nothing left soon for us poor women. I used to make hammocks for Government, but Government's getting them done now in the prisons."

"How much did you get for the hammocks?"

"Five-and-sixpence for ten."

"How much are you paid for your coal sacks?"

"Two shillings for twelve."

"What are you doing now?"

"Nothing in the canvas line. Maybe you'll come in."

The Commissioner complimented her on the neatness of the kitchen; and she said, "I like to keep a bit near the mark if I can; but I don't know what will become of us if I can't get a job. I was sitting at the door, hoping a neighbour would call me in to do a bit of washing. I've a little girl in there" (pointing to a door) "light-headed with scarlet fever, and I thought if the neighbours came in and heard her, they'd be afraid to give me any washing"

The Commissioner pointed out the doubtful morality of this conduct; but the answer was, One's own come first, and my little girl wants what I can't give her. So don't you tell of me to

School Board ; I thought from what he said you'd a job to give me."

She looked very much disappointed when our Commissioner went away. Like many other women, she was anxious to know *why* we are making this inquiry. Of course our Commissioners can only say the truth, which is that we hope, if public opinion is directed towards home industries, something may be done for these unfortunate women.

But we are not very sanguine.

One of the greatest hardships of palm-workers consists in carrying loads backwards and forwards. Some carry on the head, some on the hip. The tarpaulins are especially heavy, and women may be seen staggering beneath them in some districts. They say that the loads make them feel "light-headed ;" but as the tar is healthy it has "no fevers attached to it."

Mending old sacks is better paid, because the work is so very unpleasant. This is done at home, and also in the markets. Canvas work is much better paid in manufactories than at home. Women can make 12*s.* a week, or 2*s.* 6*d.* a day as palm-workers in manufactories.

CHAPTER IV.

BRUSH-MAKERS.

ALL sorts of brushes are made by girls and women at home; tooth-brushes, hair-brushes, dairy, churn, scrubbing, stove, shoe, stable, and even scavenger brushes pass through the hands of female workers. The work is generally carried home from a factory; but sometimes the brushes are made on the premises, if a father or brother is there to turn the backs and handles, and to sell the goods afterwards.

A Commissioner visited a girl near Lisson Grove who makes hearth-brushes for a large factory It was ten o'clock, and the girl was clearing away the breakfast. She was tall and slight, with a delicate complexion, and large liquid grey eyes. Her father stood at the door when the Commissioner went in, and she beckoned to him. The Commissioner could not hear what she said, but the man looked extremely sulky. Then the girl asked if the Commissioner wanted a brush, and said that her brother would be back in a minute.

"I know as much as he does," the father said, in a sulky voice. "I was born in the brush-making, I was, and I brought you both up to it. He's taking the work away from me, he is."

The girl slipped a penny into the man's hand, and with a growl he left the room, saying that he would come back for dinner.

"Dinner!" exclaimed the girl, after he had departed, "I'd like to know where it will come from. I'm keeping us all three," she continued; "my brother can't get a job, and I'm doing brushes to keep us. If it weren't for mother I'd give in, but mother's away in the country."

"What is she doing there?" inquired the Commissioner.

"She's dying," the girl said. "And father's took to drink since he's been out of work, and Tom, that's my brother, he can't get work. He'll be in directly."

The Commissioner sat down to wait for Tom; and while she was waiting the girl set to work. She had a job on hand—namely, a dozen hearth-brushes to make for a factory. A dozen pieces of wood lay on a table in the window, and a large quantity of fibre. The implements consisted of a vice to hold the brush while she was working at it, and a large pair of shears with which to cut the fibre after it had been passed through the holes in the wood, and secured at the back with wire. She wore a piece of leather round her right hand, about which the wire was twisted ; and with the left hand she picked up the fibre which she passed through the holes in the wood. Each piece of wood had 109 holes in it, which holes had been punched before she carried the brushes home to fill them in with fibre. The fibre and wire were provided, so her work consisted simply of wiring.

"How much will you receive for those brushes ?" inquired the Commissioner.

"Sixpence. They're a halfpenny each. They take a lot of time, and they're that troublesome, I'd never do 'em but for mother. And since she has been away in the country I've had to do the house-work as well. It's difficult to make dinners out of nothing."

"Do you ever get paid better than that ?"

"Yes, I've had as much as a penny for 100 holes ; but a halfpenny is what we get at most places. Tom does the fetching and carrying back ; so I can sit at brush-making all day when I've done the house-work."

Tom came in, and his sister explained that the visitor wanted a brush. His face lighted up as he opened the door of his small workshop. "I've had nothing to do this fortnight," he said, "so I've no money to buy wood or fibre let alone hair. I'll be happy to make the brush if you'll give me money to get the materials. I can put your initials on the handle if you like. I've made all sorts of brushes. I was born in the brush business." Then he expatiated on the hardness of his lot, and said that it went against the grain to see his sister slaving all day at brushes for the factory. "Every Englishman ought to be able to earn enough to keep himself and some one else," he said, "a sister or a missus. My sister takes after my mother, and it's just killing her to sit working all day and a good bit of the night; and it maddens me to have nothing to do but carry her work to the factory and fetch more back. She can get plenty to do, and sometimes I help her with the wiring; but it's not work for a man, and I'm clumsy at it."

The history of the father is worth repeating, as cases like his occur every day, and add to the sum of human misery. He was out of work for a year, and during that time he became weak and ill. When at last he had a job given to him the work came with a rush, and he had not strength to do it. He went to a public-house and drank some gin, which gave him strength for the job he was obliged to finish. The habit has grown upon him, and now he could not work if he had the chance; but for his daughter he must go into the workhouse.

Our Commissioners say that in many of the homes which they have visited, young girls have had black bottles beside them out of which they have been drinking. Their answer to queries is, "I'm so weak, it helps me to go on a bit." No one who visits these girls can speak severely about this habit; for the work is such hard labour, that many of the poor things are completely exhausted before they begin the day. The rooms in which they sit are small and comfortless, and their work is very monotonous.

Brush-makers live in Hackney, Southwark, Homerton, and other districts. The work is paid by the number of holes; and our Commissioners have not come across one woman who earns a decent living by brush-making. Sometimes, when the husband or father helps, it is possible to make a profit; but when the women fetch the work from factories they get little money.

A Commissioner reports six small girls in Shoreditch who stick pins in india-rubbers for brushes. They receive *2d.* for one dozen india-rubbers; and each india-rubber must have at least four hundred pins stuck into it. These india-rubbers measure four inches by two inches. The work is tiresome, but not unpleasant. The six little girls enjoy it, for the money they get goes into their own pockets, and they do it during their dinner hour, and on half-holidays. But it is a different thing when a woman has to earn her living by brush-making.

A young woman who lives in Whitechapel was visited. She had no work on hand, and was crying bitterly when our Commissioner arrived at her door. Her husband sat by the washing-stand, with his head buried in his arms, and without any coat on his back. His wife had just pawned the coat to buy food for the family; hence the cause of her tears. A loaf of bread stood on the table, and a teapot. In the arms of the young woman was a baby. Another child lay ill in bed with measles. She was able to make seven shillings a week when work came in "regular," she told the Commissioner, although it was difficult to do much with two little ones. But lately she had had no work; and her husband was "just like the rest of the men," namely, unable to find employment.

"When I get a job we'll be able to take his coat out of pawn, and he'll go on looking," the wife said. "He wears out a deal of shoe-leather going about the streets, and unless he looks a bit up to the mark he's not got a chance."

It may be worth while to quote a case reported by a Commissioner in Hackney, that of a man with grey hair, who had been constantly turned away by employers as "past work." He was advised by our Commissioner to dye his hair; and the result is that he has been taken on at one of the places where he was refused on account of his middle-aged appearance.

The dearth of work for men forces them to turn their hand to home industries; and the consequence is bitter complaints among the women, who think that the men have no right to enter this special branch of labour. The men complain of the women, the women complain of the men, and both complain of the children.

In order to see the smallest home industries it is necessary to visit the common lodging-houses. In these, at night, men and women, boys and girls, may be found busy at all sorts of small trades, making paper-bags, wooden ornaments, paper flowers, and cheap toys to be sold in the streets for a farthing or a halfpenny. A Commissioner reports a curious incident which she witnessed in Shoreditch. In a common lodging-house kitchen, where the sixty inhabitants of the place were busy at supper or work, three or four Salvation lasses walked in, and began to sing a hymn. The people took little notice, but went on with their work or their supper while the girls were singing. Presently a Salvation lass began to speak about heaven and hell, and became so excited that she waved her arms above her head, and swung them in front and behind without heeding passers-by. A poor toy-maker was carrying his merchandise out of the room, and she swept the tray from his hands in her energetic appeal to the Deity. The man made no complaint, but quietly picked up his goods, some of which were broken past repair. "Never mind, sister," he said, when the slum lassie paused to say that she was sorry, "but next time you preach keep your arms quiet."

FISH-CURING.

Curing fish is largely practised in Stepney. Fish-yards may be found there in which work goes on all the year round, and every day of the week, including Sunday. The fish is fetched from Billingsgate to be dried and taken back again when finished. Friday is the best day to see this work, for then the yards are full of fish. These yards are barns, attached to the houses at the back, and covered with tiles or straw. They are generally a few inches deep in water, and the women stand on boxes or stools while preparing the fish. "Let off the water," the owner of the yard says, and then the salt stuff is allowed to run into a sink, or out upon the street. It would be impossible to give details concerning this work, for much of it is very disgusting. An old man said to a Commissioner who visited half-a-dozen yards, "I guess you'll never eat a bit of dried fish again after what you've seen; not even a bit of salmon."

All sorts of fish are cured in these places—salmon, herrings, cod, and sprats, but chiefly haddock. The heads of the fish are cut off, the bodies are cleaned and dipped in salt-water. They are then strung on iron bars, and hung up to dry. The drying takes about five hours. Salmon are dried with coke fires first, then with oak or deal dust. Smaller fish do not require coke. The cupboards in which the fish are hung up to dry reach to the rafters of the fish-yards, and hold thousands of fish at once. The fires are generally lighted about 6 p.m., and the fish is taken down at about 4 a.m. the following morning. It is then packed in hampers and sent back to the market. Norwegian salmon is cured in large quantities, and this does not give much trouble; but each sprat must pass six times through the hands of a worker.

The work is very cold in winter. The girls say that icicles often hang from their fingers after they have dipped the fish in the salt water, and that hanging up the fish to dry in the hot cupboards gives them chilblains. They are assisted by men and boys, who carry the hampers and hang the fish on the highest bars in the cupboards. Sometimes daughters help their father and mother, and the whole work of the yard is performed by one family. The usual pay is *2s. 6d.* or *3s.* a day for the girls and women, but the work is not certain; just now it is very slack. The women say that the fish business is falling away like other industries, and that the owners of fish-yards can "only just scrape along." "It's well enough if your husband's doing something, but it's a poor thing to keep a family by," the owner of a fish-yard told our Commissioner.

Here again the women work while the men remain idle. The streets are full of youths who have no employment, who lounge on doorsteps. The habit of idleness grows upon these youths, and the women complain, "They're getting that used to hanging about with their hands in their pockets, they think it a hardship to lift a jug of water." It is impossible to lay too great stress on the demoralising influence which enforced idleness has upon these young men. The evil increases every day; and the only people who profit by it are the publicans, into whose dens the men drop in order to kill time and drown misery.

CHAPTER V.

FUR-PULLERS

THIS industry is very little known to the general public, but a great many girls and women earn their living by it in Bermondsey and other metropolitan districts. The most unpleasant part of the work consists in pulling the skins of rabbits—namely, in rubbing the loose down off them with a blunt knife, which process prepares them for lining cloaks and jackets. The down is returned to the furrier, who uses it to stuff beds, sofas, and pillows. A fur-puller explained to a Commissioner that this fur is "handsome for rheumatics." Fur-pullers formerly received 1*s.* 9*d.* per five dozen skins; but now so many women have gone into the business that only 1*s.* 1*d.* is generally paid for that quantity. This fur-pulling cannot be done by machinery at present. At the time of the Crimean war a great many women became fur-pullers, for large numbers of rabbit-skins were then wanted to line the coats of soldiers. Now the skins are chiefly used for the cloaks and jackets of women and children. The work is very unpleasant. The fur-puller sits in a small barn, or out-house, on a low stool. She has a trough in front of her, into which she drops the down as she pulls it off the rabbit-skins with her knife. Occasionally she stops to rub the knife with whiting, for the skins are greasy. The down gets into her nose and mouth. Her hair and clothes are white with it. She generally suffers from what she calls "breathlessness," for her lungs are filled with the fine down, and she is always more or less choked.

Another branch of the fur-pulling business consists in cutting open the tails of rabbits in order to extract the little bone in the middle. The bones are returned to the manufacturer, who sells them for manure. The fur is paid by the lb., and the worker generally receives 8*d.* per lb. for it after the bones have been extracted. This fur is used to make cheap blankets, and those fur hats which are sold at such low prices. Old pieces of rabbit-skins are also used for these purposes. One fur-puller in the Borough who has been visited by our Commissioners, receives 9*d.* per lb. for preparing old pieces of skins. Her daughter works at the same business. When the Commissioner went into their room, the two women were found sitting at a small table, which was covered with skins and tails. Each woman had a strong pair of scissors, with which to clip the fur from the skin. Large paper bags stood on the floor, ready to receive the down. The bed was strewed with skins, and the floor was littered with small bones. The place smelt of dead rabbit, and the air was thick with fine white hairs. These fur-pullers were not communicative; but they vouchsafed to say that it was difficult to make a living by fur-pulling.

PIPE-MAKING.

Another large home industry is that of making clay pipes. These are generally bought by publicans at 1*s.*, 1*s.* 6*d.*, or 2*s.* per gross to give away in the public-houses. If a customer buys tobacco, he receives a clay pipe with it as a present. Such pipes frequently have the mark of the house or the initials of the publican upon them. But cigarettes are taking their place. Young men prefer cigarettes to pipes, and can buy five in a box at the bar for a penny. Clay pipes are difficult to make, and require a great deal of practice. Sixteen must be made to the dozen, for many break, and many are imperfect.

The clay is bought by the ton. It takes a good deal of time to prepare, and when prepared must pass through at least six processes. First of all it is shaped; secondly, a wire is run through the stem; thirdly, the bowl is formed in a mould; fourthly, it is dried; fifthly, it is trimmed; sixthly, it is baked. The mould costs about 30*s.*, and each public-house has its own mould, unless the publican is poor. The drying is done over a slow fire, and afterwards the pipes must be carefully tried to see if they will draw properly. Many break in the kiln. Last of all, the mouthpieces are painted with sealing-wax. And after all this, the pipes are sold at less than a farthing each!

We do not intend to notice many more of these home industries. Those we have already placed before our readers show that most of the work is done at a starvation rate of payment. Of course there are places in which women and girls are well paid. Thus one who has been eighteen years in the fancy-box trade wrote to tell us that he has in his employ "hands" who in their own homes earned from 12*s.* to 15*s.* a week at the fancy-box business. He wished our Commissioners to visit a firm in the City Road, where two hundred girls and women make fancy boxes, because he has seen these people wearing kid gloves and velvet dresses. Our Commissioners have only visited those engaged in home industries. We said that some box-makers are well paid, and that some are paid at a lower rate than those match-box-makers about whose work such a bitter cry was raised before we began our inquiry. Small boxes are made to hold powder at 2*d.* the gross in many London districts. These consist merely of the tray that goes inside a common matchbox. Our correspondent says that no "hand," be she ever so quick, could make more than one gross of collar boxes in a day, and the price would be at least 2*s.* per gross. This is no doubt true of workers who wear velvet dresses and kid gloves. It is quite a different thing where people are starving, for the work of such "hands" goes on all night as well as all day.

While the public continues to take an interest in the sweating system, it is well to call attention to these home industries. True, the girls and women do not always receive their work through middle-men, but in the sweat of their faces they eat bread. People know so little about them that the Lords' Committee is not likely to give them help. Perhaps they are better without such assistance. There is no doubt that when the Lords' inquiry is finished, many witnesses will be quietly sacked by their employers. This will not be done at once; but within a year, or six months, excuses will be made for getting rid of them. However willing these witnesses may be then to sweat, no sweater will give them the chance of sweating. They will be marked men and women. Thus it may be well that the home industries should remain dark at present.

There is a plan on foot to open an exhibition of home industries, at which a number of specimens will be exhibited. Such specimens are being collected with considerable circumspection, and in secrecy, in order that the employées may not be involved in difficulties. What the employers will say if the plan succeeds it is difficult to think, for their property is finding its way into collectors' pockets, and they will see a variety of their purloined articles exhibited to an astonished public. This might perhaps bring home to consumers the state of producers more graphically than can be done by writing. Thus a lady would learn that the tooth-brush which she uses morning and evening passed through the hands of a starving girl; that the sofa on which she lies is stuffed with rabbit-down that has stifled a poor widow: that the ball with which she plays tennis came from a room in which children lay ill with scarlet fever. People sometimes wonder how epidemics creep into carefully guarded households. They quite forget that the vermin and small-pox, of which they are so much afraid that they carefully avoid the slums of the metropolis, come to them through these home industries. A parish doctor told a Commissioner that he had seen badges for soldiers' uniforms being made in rooms where children had infectious complaints, and that the germs might thus be carried into barracks. These badges ruin the eyes of workers, and are paid at a low rate. A Commissioner visited a poor girl who does them, and found her eyes in a shocking condition. The eyes of a young woman who makes snaps for crackers are even worse, and this woman's child is almost blind, thanks to the stuff which is put into the snaps. It is terrible to think that the crackers which excite so much merriment among rich children are produced at such a cost by their poorer sisters. The woman, who was visited, receives 1*s.* 9*d.* per day for twelve hours' work. She cuts the cardboard into narrow strips, and puts between two bits of it some stuff made of silver, nitric acid, sand, and methylated spirits. The snaps are then covered with paper, dried, and tied up in packets. This industry is being superseded by snaps from Germany, and women can scarcely make a living at it, even with the assistance of their children.

Home industries include paper flowers, fans, rag dolls, arms and legs of dolls, baskets, shell ornaments, boxes for sweets, frames, brackets, lace, chains, etc., etc. Umbrellas are now made by machinery, but the elastic bands for them are done by women at home. These consist of button, ring, and flap. They are paid at 4*d.* per gross. The tops of tassels are worked by women, and are paid at 4*s.* 6*d.* per gross. One gross takes a week to make, for the work is fine and troublesome. Bead trimming of all sorts is done at home by girls and women. Our Commissioners have visited a girl who makes blackberry-trimming. This is paid at 1*s.* 6*d.* per gross of blackberries, and the girl can do one gross in the day; by this work she has brought up a family of brothers and sisters. She lost her mother when the youngest child was two years old, and with the help of an elder brother she has kept the home together. The brother is now married; but she keeps on the one room in which they have all lived for ten years, and still works at the bead business. When asked if she meant to marry, she shook her head, and said, "I've no time for courting."

Weaving has died out in many districts, but sometimes our Commissioners have come across women with looms. One old lady near Drury Lane says that she made binding for the Queen's carriages at the Jubilee. Her Majesty little thinks when she leans back in one of these carriages whose hands wove the binding of her cushions. The binding was of Oxford and Cambridge blue. The poor woman received 2½*d.* per yard for it. She produced about six yards a day, by working from dawn till dark. She told our Commissioner that her employer always made a favour of giving her work, and said it was just to keep her out of the workhouse. "But I know better," she continued. "Hand-work's better than machine-work. That's why he gave me the job for the Jubilee." She is bent almost double, and her right arm is broken. Her chest is sunken, and her knuckles are swollen. For thirty-six years she had inhabited the same room. She pays for it 2*s.* 6*d.*, and half of it is filled with the great loom, at which she works all the year round without any holiday. In one window is a creeping-jenny, which she bought at a

Sunday market for *6d.*; in the other is a single grain of wheat, planted in an old whelk-shell.

We shall notice later on those women who make shirts, coats, and waistcoats in their own houses, all of which come under the heading of home industries. Buttonhole makers have already attracted the notice of the public, and this work is often quoted, together with the making of match-boxes, when a bitter cry finds its way into a meeting or a newspaper. A poor woman in Southwark was visited who supports herself and five children by making buttonholes at $2\frac{3}{4}$*d.* per gross. A woman in the same house makes bows for boys at 10*d.* per gross. Neckties are not paid much better.

Every day more women compete for these home industries. The wives and daughters of clerks do much of this work *sub rosa*, and actually undersell the poorer women. They thus try to eke out the small incomes of husbands and fathers. On few people does the Juggernaut competition place a heavier foot than clerks. Their wives can tell tales of economies which make the lives of beggars in the streets appear luxurious. Beggars are not obliged to keep up an appearance, without which many clerks must starve or go into the workhouse. The wives of these men are much to be pitied : but they get a good deal of pleasure out of their would-be "gentility," and if the shoe pinches they console themselves with the thought that some people go shoeless.

CHAPTER VI.

SLAVEYS.

IT is stated that one-half of the three and a half millions of women and girls engaged in industrial employment throughout the United Kingdom are in domestic service. How many of these domestics are " slaveys " it is impossible to say. By a " slavey " we mean a child-servant, a Maria, Jane, or Susan, who drudges from morning till night in some house where " only one servant is kept." Of course we are speaking here of metropolitan slaveys, those, for instance, who come under the notice of societies like the M.A.B.Y.S. How many slaveys there are in London at present it is impossible to say; but the M.A.B.Y.S. (Metropolitan Association for Befriending Young Servants) has under its care at least 8,000 slaveys, and other societies such as the Girls' Friendly Society, the Young Women's Christian Association, the Girls' Helpful Society, etc., etc., have the names of many girls on their books.

Readers must not think that our inquiry into the condition of slaveys has been confined to the work of these societies. Our Commissioners have worked independently of any organisation. They have visited the girls in their homes, and in their situations. They have even made the experiment of placing a slavey in a gentleman's house, in order to see for themselves what can, under the most favourable circumstances, be made of a child-servant. But as more seems to be done by societies and charities for slaveys than for any other class of young women in London, we think it advisable to notice the work of the M.A.B.Y.S. before we pass on to particular cases. This Asso ciation is worked upon such excellent principles that scarcely any other agency would be needed for slaveys if only it were in communication with the Board schools as well as with the pauper schools of the metropolis.

It divides the girls under its care into two branches. One class embraces destitute and friendless girls, who are handed over to the care of the Association when discharged from the pauper schools; the other class consists of local girls who apply to the various branches of the Association for situations. The pauper girls are friendless and homeless after they leave school.

Our Commissioners report the case of a pauper girl whose history we give by way of illustration. This girl was fetched from the workhouse by a lady, and kept for half a year as a slavey. Then the lady gave up her house, sold her furniture, and went abroad. She put an advertisement in a paper before she went to find the girl a place. This was answered by a lady at St. John's Wood The girl was sent there with her box. It was a bad house. The girl got away with difficulty. She applied for a situation at the —— Hotel, where servants are taken without characters. When the proprietor heard that she was "in trouble," he dismissed her at a moment's notice. She then went to the —— Hospital. There a young doctor took pity on her. He gave her money to find a lodging, and put her into communication with a lady who is interested in such cases. This lady found the girl in a house near Baker Street, and wrote to her former mistress. The mistress was horrified when she heard what had taken place, and sent money to help the girl through her difficulties. But she did not seem to see that her negligence had brought about the mischief, or to realise that a workhouse girl is one of the most friendless creatures on the face of the earth if the M.A.B.Y.S. does not happen to make her acquaintance.

6

The M.A.B.Y.S. has branches all over London; and mistresses who have child-servants should communicate with the Association if they have not time to find places for discharged slaveys. Small charities, too, would do well to put themselves in communication with the Association.

A Commissioner reports the following case, which came under her notice last December. She was walking through Onslow Gardens at 5 p.m. one evening. There she saw a girl crying on the doorstep. This girl had been dismissed from a small Home for striking a companion, and had been turned out into the street with a shilling, and the address of a convent at Shepherd's Bush. The Commissioner took the girl back to the Home, and begged the superintendent to receive her for the night, as it was getting dark. The superintendent refused, although the girl was a stranger in London, and did not know her way to the Metropolitan Railway. The Commissioner then went with the girl to the clergyman of the parish, who handed her over to the workhouse authorities.

The metropolis is, as every one knows, divided into thirty-two unions. The guardians of most of these workhouses send the names and addresses of the girls who leave the pauper schools to the Association. The girls are then placed in communication with one of the branches of the Association, and generally under the care of a lady visitor. No one can say how much good has been done by the intimate relationship which exists between these lady visitors and the friendless pauper servants.

An excellent pamphlet on the subject, entitled "The Work of the Lady Visitors," has been written by Mrs. S. A. Barnett. She speaks of the dislike which some mistresses evince towards lady visitors, and advises the visitors to write to the mistress for permission to call on Mary Jane or Susan, instead of knocking at the door and demanding to see the slavey. She says that the first visit should always be paid *to the mistress.*

"As a rule," says Mrs. Barnett, "when properly prepared by a judicious note, the mistress receives the lady visitor cordially, looks upon her as an assistance in the management of her servant, pours into her ears (we hope not such unwilling ones) a tale of woes as long as the Ancient Mariner's, and asks her to rebuke her servant for all the faults which she either has not the courage or the force of character to attack. In many cases she receives the lady gladly, as a friend to her girl, as one to whom she can turn to bring some brightness into the life of the hard-worked little maid, for whom the mistress has an honest liking, and whom she herself would make happy, if her means were not limited by poverty, ignorance, a large family, and much work. In either case, permission for the girl to visit the lady, or for the lady to repeat her visit to the girl, is generally given, and that granted, the work is—*only* to hold the girl, to win her heart.

"It is not a difficult task this, to win a girl's heart—in the case of the pauper girls a touchingly easy one. The girl, brought up in an enormous school, with teachers to teach, nurses to nurse, mistresses to order, no one to love; launched into the world at an age when the heart and mind are awakening into life, when the capability for joy or sorrow is most keen; sent out into a bewildering world, as Mrs. Browning says,

> "'Suddenly awake to full life and life's needs and agonies,
> With an intense, strong, struggling heart'—

so ignorant of life's common ways and ordinary conditions, that right gets confused with wrong; so painfully new to all the surroundings that the newness hurts; with no past to help the future; no memories of a wise tender mother, whose words of counsel must now be taken, having before been proven true; with no practical knowledge of principles which *must* be clung to whatever is abandoned; with no friend bound up with girlish joys—only a school in the past. It is the heart of such a girl, empty because no one has cared to fill it, which is given over to the lady to win, and it is this girl, whose character comes to us as 'sullen, obstinate, and sly,' whose eyes at the first word of kindness fill with tears—tears hitherto rarely summoned, except by physical pain—it is this girl, whose interest once awakened, lives on the memory of your words, to whom you can become, in an awe-inspiring way, a conscience."

Mrs. Barnett goes on to speak of the methods which a visitor should use to help the girl and win her friendship. Savings can be discussed, and the girl can be taught to "lay by" a little money; difficulties in the way of work can be talked over, also the management of the children who are entrusted to the slavey.

"But it is not well always to talk of the girl's own affairs," says Mrs. Barnett. "It should, I think, be the visitor's duty to give the girl a wider view of life, to interest her in other people's aims, to teach her to care for those whose lot is sadder and more full of pain than her own."

Thus books can be lent and magazines, and the girl is interested in and induced to spend odd minutes working for others.

Mrs. Barnett recommends the visitors to procure holidays for the slaveys, and on these rare occasions to invite the girls to their own homes, and to take their *protegées* to the Crystal Palace, or some other place of amusement. People little think how the memories of such days live on in the minds of slaveys.

Our Commissioners report a little servant in South Hackney who was taken to the National Gallery, and then to a house in Chelsea. When the child reached the National Gallery her eyes remained fixed on the floors, and she did not look at the pictures. "My! how these 'ere floors must make some one's arms ache," she said. "It would kill me to scrub 'em entirely."

She was so overwhelmed by the amount of hard manual labour those floors represented that the pictures failed to attract her notice. When she was asked at the end of the day what had pleased her most, she said, "I liked that museum best, the one your friend lives in."

This was the drawing-room of a lady in Chelsea where she had tea. She talks still of that "museum" to her brothers and sisters; also of the floors at the National Gallery. Her mother pulled her right arm out of its socket in a drunken fit when she was an infant; consequently she finds scrubbing a painful occupation, even in the small abode of her mistress.

Mrs. Barnett gives advice to visitors on the subject of "sweethearts," which all should read who are interested in young servants. The pamphlet can be obtained from the Secretary of the Society, or from Messrs. Sothern and Co., 36, Piccadilly. Few ladies know more about slaveys than Mrs. Barnett, who has interested herself in them for years. In fact, the work of sending young girls into service is carried on to such an extent in St. Jude's parish that the mothers have more than once complained to our Commissioners of well-meant interference.

As we said before, the M.A.B.Y.S. does not only look after pauper girls, but all those who apply to it for assistance. Each branch has a free registry office, to which local girls can come who want situations; and when they are once settled in service a lady visitor is appointed to look after them. Friendship is the principle of the Association, not profit. Clothing clubs are also attached to the branches, and the girls receive outfits for service, which they repay by instalments from their wages. Training and lodging homes are also in connection with the Association, for the assistance of friendless girls and strangers to the metropolis. The organisation of the Association is very thorough, and *could* include the whole of London. As the Bishop of Chichester says, "The multiplication of charitable institutions is in itself an evil. There ought to be a better organisation of existing charity." This is especially true with regard to young servants. For no class of girls in London is so much done as for "slaveys;" and if the charities were better organised, if they worked with that charitable feeling which makes all men brethren, no slavey need feel herself neglected. One step in the right direction would be to affiliate all the Board schools with the M.A.B.Y.S., as most of the pauper schools are affiliated. Each school-mistress should send a list of girls leaving school to the branch of the Association in her district. Then the girls would be visited before they have time to drift into day-maids (about whom we shall have more to say presently), to become "hands" in factories and shops, or to begin the hundred and one small occupations which lead to nothing. A girl who applies for a place on her own account has a poor chance in service. She needs clothes and a character.

"The chap I keep company with will speak up for me," a girl told a Commissioner the other day. She was quite surprised to hear that this was not likely to win her a place with an ordinary mistress.

The situations which slaveys can get through the small metropolitan registry offices are not generally very satisfactory; and even in these want of clothes prevents many a girl from getting any sort of situation.

It has been suggested that registry offices and clothing clubs might be attached to Board schools, and that if the mistresses were too busy to attend to such things, the clergyman's wife or the district visitors could do the work. It would be much better to send a list of girls about to leave school to the local branch of the M.A.B.Y.S. at the end of each term. If this were done by all the Board schools, the girls would be looked after and prepared for service.

Many mothers, however, like to keep their girls at home for a year or two before letting them go into service. Such people think, "If I've got a daughter I may as well get the benefit." They say that the School Board is hard on mothers; and directly the girls are old enough to leave school they make them into home drudges. But the girls often rebel against this, and sometimes give their mothers "notice." Or they get into bad company, and the mothers think that they would be safer in service. The mothers then take their girls to the M.A.B.Y.S., if they know of it, and ask the ladies to find their daughters places. Of course the girls who pass straight from school into service make the best servants.

We have spoken at length about the M.A.B.Y.S., because it is the slaveys' Association *par excellence;* and there is no doubt that if its branches were affiliated with the Board schools, properly organised, and well supported, the Association could easily cover all the work that has to be done among this class of young women in London.

CHAPTER VII.

SLAVEYS.

(Continued.)

LONDON girls of the lowest class have a strong prejudice against domestic service. Mothers are, as a rule, glad to see their girls in "a tidy little place." They realise that good food is necessary for a girl while she is growing, and that street life is very pernicious. But the girls often prefer to live at home, even if it means drudgery that keeps them occupied from morning till night, blows, and drunken parents. The routine of service tries them very much, and they miss the companionship of school friends, brothers and sisters. They complain of "lonesomeness."

A girl was visited lately by our Commissioners who had run away from her first place, and entered a factory. When asked why she had done this, she said, "Well, missus always sat in the parlour, and I always sat in the kitchen, and I felt lonesome. Then missus used to go out at night, and leave me all alone in the house, and I got scared, and runned away. I won't go back," she added, "no, not for nobody."

Girls of this class are accustomed to live in one or two rooms, with father, mother, brothers and sisters. So when they suddenly find themselves in a strange place at night, alone, in the dark, they become nervous; and if the mistress places an impassable barrier between the parlour and the kitchen, the child-servant mopes, gives notice, or runs away, unless she has the true soul of a slavey.

Pauper girls make, as a rule, very good servants. Their spirit is broken by long and severe discipline before they leave the workhouse. They seldom complain of anything. But the girl who has tasted the sweets of liberty is apt to run away, if she becomes a slavey. It is not the work which she minds so much as the "lonesomeness."

The girl who was placed six months ago in the house of Major ——, —— Street, Kensington, is a fair type of the ordinary slavey. Her father rents two cellars near Lisson Grove. He is out of work, and only able to scrape along with the assistance of his wife, who is a charwoman. He has six children. The eldest girl works in a factory, and earns four shillings and sixpence per week. Sarah is nearly fifteen, but looks like a child of twelve, because she is small and thin, the result of constant starving. Her father is a very respectable man, although out of work, having been employed in a shop for many years. He now does odd jobs and runs errands. He was very anxious to find Sarah "a tidy little place," and delighted that she should go to service. The day on which this was arranged the mother lay in bed with the two youngest children because her clothes were in the pawnshop. The father had applied for relief to the parish. So money was given to buy Sarah some clothes; and the girl was transported from her wretched home to the house in Kensington. At first she was delighted with everything. She worked hard, and tried "to give satisfaction." The father called, and seemed pleased to see the child so happy. But from the first she complained of "lonesomeness." She would not answer the back-door bell after dark, or sleep by herself. She cried when the cook left her alone in the kitchen. Then she began to mope, and said that she wanted her brothers and sisters, that she was sure her mother was ill, and that she felt ill herself. She begged for pocket-money, saying that her mother had given her a few pence on a Saturday night. She asked to go out by herself, instead of with another servant. Last of all she ran away, having received a shilling from some one in the house, and permission from the cook to fetch a stamp. She preferred her wretched home, in which she had not enough to eat, to the house in Kensington, and now works ten hours a day in a factory, and gets two shillings and sixpence a week. She received the kindest treatment, and her life in the house of Major —— was very different to that of most slaveys. But she was home-sick. Let readers picture the lives of pauper servants, who have no homes ; and then think of the little Mary Jane or Susan to whom " the terrors of the night season " come again and again, as they lie awake in the garret or mope in the kitchen. These children are made of flesh and blood, although they are servants.

There is no difficulty in persuading London girls to go out as " day-maids," namely, from eight o'clock in the morning until eight o'clock at night. Then they sleep at home ; they are not separated from their brothers and sisters. If a girl is asked, after she leaves school, " What would you like to do ? " she generally says, " Please I'd like to mind a baby."

Many girls act as nurses to the children of neighbours, or to small shopkeepers, and earn about two shillings and sixpence a week. Sometimes dinner is included, but generally the girl only receives her tea from the family. Many girls in the East End are employed by well-to-do Jewesses, and pass from house to house, receiving pence and scraps in return for scrubbing and washing up. The M.A.B.Y.S. sets its face against day-servants, for they are out late at night, and under the charge of neither mother nor mistress. But the girls enjoy the position of semi-independence; and it is remarkable to witness how different the manner of a slavey is to that of a day-servant. The latter is much the most independent.

Slaveys receive from £5 to £7 a year as wages. Out of this they have to buy clothes, boots and shoes, and to provide for a variety of small expenses. Girls in lodging-houses do not receive so much, for they are supposed to have perquisites. It is a commonly understood thing among Irish servants that if their wages are not what they consider sufficient, pilfering has the blessing of the priest, or at any rate he winks at it. The same idea seems to exist in the minds of most landladies. Of course there are many exceptions; but that the ordinary landlady is a parasite who expects her lodgers to keep her in food and raiment, and to pay her rent, is well known to the public Thus she helps herself to the lodger's tea and sugar, she takes a little bit of his butter, she shares his bread, and she lets the cat eat his cold mutton. She charges for his coal three times as much as she pays herself; and if he does not complain, she calls him "quite the gentleman." Thus he hears his landlady say to the slavey, "Susan, bring down Mr. ——'s tea-caddy," and if he ventures to remonstrate, Susan says, "Missus didn't know as you were in the house, sir."

For the sake of peace and a quiet life he allows his landlady to fleece him; and in time he becomes so abject that he is afraid to "give notice." No wonder that he *feels* for the slavey. He hears the landlady scolding Susan, and afterwards he gives Susan sixpence. Much of his comfort depends on the little maid-servant. She cleans his boots, and brings him hot water; she answers his bell, and prepares his breakfast. Her dirty face and draggled dress seem to be part and parcel of his cheap lodgings; her very curl-papers are familiar, also her dirty apron. Only she is for ever changing! It is always the same tale, "I can't put up with the missus." Then another girl takes her place; and the other girl "gives notice."

A Commissioner visited a slavey in a large lodging-house near the City, in which there are thirty lodgers, including clerks who earn £2 a week. This child, aged fourteen, does the whole of the work, with the assistance of an old half-daft man who came to the house as a lodger, and stayed on to "give a hand" whenever he was wanted. The girl sleeps in the kitchen, which is downstairs. Her bed is kept in the kitchen cupboard. She gets up at five o'clock, and slaves all day long for the lodgers. She cleans and dusts, she carries up water, she helps cook the dinner, she answers the bells, she never sits down except for meals. She "gets her tea standing." She has no idea who she is, or where she comes from, only a vague recollection of parents down in the country, who gave her to an aunt in London. She believes that she belongs body and soul to the "missus," who also seems to look upon the child as her personal property. She has only one pleasure in life, namely, a white cat who lives with her in the kitchen, and sleeps on her bed at night. The "missus" does the shopping; so the girl drudges all day in the lodgers' rooms, she works from top to bottom, and bottom to top, and then she begins again from the beginning.

Another girl was visited in Chelsea, who lives in the family of a comic actor. This girl has charge of three children. Her mistress complains that she falls asleep while she is dressing,and the girl says that this comes to pass because the baby is teething She is growing fast, and the heavy baby tries her strength. She must wash and dress all of the children, and get breakfast with the baby in her arms. She calls the baby "a comical little customer," and seems fond of the child, although he keeps her awake at night. She has a sweetheart, whose mother is very kind to her, and to this woman's house she goes once a month. For these Sundays she treasures up her money, in order to make a smart appearance. Her mistress is very kind, but slip-shod, and apt to leave everything to the servant.

It is useless to multiply cases. Every one knows what the life of a slavey is, for fiction and farce have made her famous.

The fathers of slaveys are generally labourers or mechanics. One of the secretaries of the M.A.B.Y.S. asserts that the girls who do best are the daughters of men who work in the large London breweries. Such men are well paid, and keep their places. "If a father has worked for some years in the same place we can always recommend the girl; we are pretty sure that she will turn out well," the same lady told our Commissioner.

No doubt the happiest slaveys are those who work for people with whom they eat their dinner, by whom they are treated as one of the family.

Those who suffer most are girls "kept at their distance" by mistresses who complain that slaveys do not see the difference between themselves and a lady. Midway between these come the lodging-house slaveys.

The lives of all these girls are dull and hard, unless they happen to have an exceptionally kind mistress, or to come under the notice of a lady visitor from the M.A.B.Y.S., or an associate of the Girls' Friendly Society. Some are sent to Sunday Schools, but mistresses think, as a rule, that girls make undesirable acquaintance in such places, and prefer to take them to church on Sunday evening, when their work is finished. Mistresses say that a visit home will upset a slavey for weeks, and that she never settles into a place if her parents are allowed to pay her visits. There are no clubs for slaveys, no rooms in which they can meet for games and music. Working girls of all sorts have clubs in London; but these girls have nothing to break the monotony of their lives except a monthly outing.

Mr. Ruskin says that a nation is in a bad way when its girls and young women are sad. If he could glance into the many suburban villas in which slaveys sit alone in the kitchen, he would think the case of London hopeless. The pauper girls who have left the workhouse. the girls whose homes are far away, may be found there by hundreds, depressed and lonely.

In conclusion, we would remind readers that a certain class of women takes its recruits chiefly from the class of young servants. Many of these arrive in London as strangers. Clergymen and people in the country who are interested in girls should communicate with the Travellers' Aid Department, 16a, Old Cavendish Street, W., which has been organised for the benefit of young women coming to London. This Society is prepared to meet any girl of whose arrival they receive three days' notice, addressed "To the Travellers' Secretary." Girls are then conducted safely to their destinations, or placed in homes and lodging-houses known to the Society. The Society has notices up in the waiting-rooms of railway stations; but it is not much known as yet in country districts.

CHAPTER VIII.

"A PERFECT SERVANT."

A COMMISSIONER was expressing regret during our inquiry that so much suspicion exists between servants and mistresses. "It is almost impossible," said the Commissioner, "to get an unbiassed opinion. Mistresses seem to think that servants are all bad, and servants shake their heads over mistresses."

This was said to three or four City gentlemen, whose office lies close to the office of THE BRITISH WEEKLY. "Well, we have *a perfect servant*," one of them remarked. "I know she must be perfect, for my wife says so; and my wife is *very* particular."

The other gentlemen said that a perfect servant presupposed a perfect mistress. They also said something about servants being made of flesh and blood, although mistresses seemed to think them bits of machinery. But their remarks were not encouraged, for gentlemen are not supposed to know anything about servants.

The perfect servant was visited forthwith; also the perfect mistress. She is eighteen years of age, a strong, well-made young woman, with beautiful hair and a bright colour. Her face glows from a plentiful supply of soap to the open pores of the skin, and much rubbing. She is a general servant—that is to say, she does all the work of the house, with a little assistance from her mistress. But the lady of the house is delicate, and consequently she leaves nearly everything to the servant, calling in a charwoman "to do extra work—like washing blankets." The family consists of master, mistress, grown-up daughter, a boy who goes to a day-school, and two little children. The house has six bedrooms, one nursery, two sitting-rooms, and two kitchens; all of which have to be "cleaned" every day, and "turned out" once a week. All the washing of the family is done by the perfect servant, "except the master's shirts." She cooks, looks after the children, scours, dusts—in fact, does all that has to be done. Her face glows with health, she expresses herself to be "perfectly happy," and she "gives satisfaction." She receives £12 a year (the wages of general servants in London vary from £12 to £18), without beer or perquisites. She goes out one evening every week, every Sunday evening, and also for a whole day every month. She is a Roman Catholic, and her mistress seems to think that the confessional-box is a safety-valve for gossip. She has no lover, but spends her free time with a married sister who lives in London. She is good-tempered honest, sober, cheerful, affectionate, hard-working. She is an early riser, very neat, makes her own clothes, and is "properly supplied with under-clothing." (This, we hear, is very rare among general servants.) She does not resent her uniform, namely, the cap and apron which so many girls refuse to put on, thinking them a badge of servitude.

"It is very difficult to get a good general servant," the lady told our Commissioner. "London girls will not go to service if they can help it, and mistresses are quite laughed at when they put their names down for general servants at the registry offices. I know ladies who have had to wait months before they were suited. The girls are so independent. Before I found this girl I was almost in despair, for the girls who applied to me made so many stipulations. One said she would consult her young man about coming in at 10 p.m. on her free evenings; but she did not think that he would fall in with such an arrangement. Another said that we were too many in family; and so it went on until I found this treasure. But servants always behave well to me. I have never had any trouble with servants.

"I think if she had a mistress who 'nagged' at her, she might show a bit of temper," the mistress said. "But so far I have never heard her say a rough word to the children, or any one else. *She is perfect.*"

It is only fair to say that the mistress of the perfect servant has never yet been obliged to give a servant "notice." Her servants have only left her for family reasons of their own, such as to get married. Yet it is not an easy place, for the two children can only just walk about, and the family consists of six people. The house is large, and fully furnished. The master likes to have his dinner cooked as becomes a City gentleman. And all the work must be done by *Saturday morning;* for the mistress wishes to devote herself then to her husband.

Among the hardships which general servants have to contend with, this lady mentioned the door-bell. "My servant is fetched from her work sometimes ten or twelve times in one morning to answer the bell," she said. "Men selling flowers and vegetables, old clothes merchants, agents, and all sorts of people come to the door. I answer the bell if I am downstairs; but the servant's legs must ache by the end of the day, for the stairs are steep, and she is generally obliged to answer it. I wonder that a spiegel * is not introduced over here, such as they have in Holland, or a small grating like those which are attached to the doors of German houses. It would save servants' time, and be a great help to mistresses."

Among the hardships of mistresses the lady spoke about the gossip which general servants indulge in. "Many servants spend their time gossiping across the garden wall with the next-door servant. If a mistress goes out she may be sure that her last dress and her next dinner will be poured into the ear of a neighbour's servant. This makes mischief, and is very unpleasant. Of course when two or three servants are kept there is not so much cause for gossip; but general servants must speak to some one. So the tittle-tattle of a street echoes along, and ends in scandal. Some mistresses listen to servants' gossip; and others who will not condescend to such things are annoyed by the constant under-current of small-talk which general servants find so pleasant."

* A spiegel is made of two pieces of looking-glass, fastened together like a book that is half-open. The glasses have a small mirror at the top, and stand on an iron rod, outside the window. Thus the inhabitants of the house can see all who pass up and down the street, and all who come to their door.

Another good general servant (if not perfect) has been reported to our Commissioner as having saved no less than £400 during twenty years of service. All this time she was in one family; and for eight years she did the whole work of a large household. She began with £14 a year for wages. Out of this she paid the rent of her seat in a Wesleyan chapel, gave liberally to charities, and dressed herself. She had no one dependent on her, so she was able to put by all that she did not require for her yearly expenses. At first she carried her money to the savings bank; but after it amounted to £100 her master took charge of it, allowing her five per cent. Before he did this an agreement was drawn up by a lawyer, and the whole thing was "legally superintended." She is stated to have had a mania for china ornaments when she first went to service (crazes for blue china, etc., are not confined to æsthetic gentlemen and ladies). But she conquered this with the help of her mistress, and is now in a fair way to "settle comfortably."

Her case is typical of the general servant in a gentleman's family. She came under the care of an excellent mistress, who treated her like "a poorer daughter." This lady told our Commissioner that "the tendency of the day is to level everything," and said that "God has made social distinctions which must be kept between classes" (at least, her words were to that effect, so far as our Commissioner can remember). The lady was taught housekeeping by an excellent servant in her grandmother's house, and is not above cooking her own dinner. In fact, she has cooked a dinner in full evening dress, and then presided at the head of her table minus her cooking apron. She very rightly thinks that as man is a cooking animal, and distinguished from the beasts by his propensity to eat flesh roasted, the daughters of men should not be ashamed to practise the art of cooking. But she says that raw meat makes her shudder, and that the fumes of the kitchen give her a headache. Nevertheless, her young daughters are to be taught housekeeping. She seems to consider that the reason why German women excel our countrywomen in happiness arises from the fact that they have daily exercise for their muscles, and they have no reason to consider themselves useless members of society. When asked how much liberty she gives to her servants, she replied, "As much as I give to my own children." In fact, the servants of this lady are under maternal government, and the result is £400 savings on the part of one who has spent twenty years in her family. It is only fair to say that when visitors came to the house all the tips went to this general servant; and as the visitors were many her purse did not wholly depend on her wages. She thinks of buying a little cottage in which to stow herself and the china ornaments that now grace her spinster fireplace.

While talking of parsimony we must quote another general servant who has saved over £500 in twenty-five years which have been spent in one family. Mistresses complain that servants use too much coal, and are careless of dripping, because they are not obliged to pay for such things, that they burn candles and "swallow matches" in a way they would not do if the money for lights came out of their own pockets. This servant lives in the family of a gentleman who has a long pedigree and a short purse. She has helped to bring up six boys on a small income. Yet she has saved over £500 herself, and she must have put thousands into her employer's pocket. The following true anecdotes will show how she has managed it.

Last year a gentleman who is well known in Parliament called to see her master. She opened the door and conducted him into the hall. Then she looked at his boots. "Please, sir," she said "will you wipe your feet? *We've* a new drawing-room carpet."

On another occasion, when the eldest brother of her mistress called in the lady's absence to say good-bye before he went to the south of France for six months, she produced at his request a postcard out of her mistress's desk. When he returned to England half a year later, she asked him, "Mr. ——, sir, have you paid back that postcard to the mistress?"

Scores of such stories could be repeated by the boys she has brought up. They call her "the heiress," and it is an open secret that the Benjamin of the family will one day have her money.

Many mistresses complain that general servants spend too much money on dress. Materials are very cheap, ribbons and feathers can be had for a few pence. Dressmakers make costumes for servants at a low rate of payment. Added to these facts are the following truths, which help to explain a general servant's extravagance. One day in the month is her own, and perhaps two afternoons in the week. She counts the hours between these periods as a school girl counts the days to the holidays. For these few hours she hoards her finery, in order to produce an impression on her acquaintances. Every one knows that soldiers in London let themselves out by the hour on Sundays, and that the price varies from 1*s.* to 5*s.* per hour for a good-looking soldier.

Most general servants have sweethearts—some "friend" with whom they walk and talk, without thinking much about marriage. While the lives of general servants remain what they are at present, such people will spend money on their appearance, unless their mistresses bring to bear on them personal influence, or they become engaged to some respectable man for whom they have a real liking. There is not the smallest doubt that general servants are, as a rule, extravagant and improvident; but these things arise largely from their position in the houses as dependents, people who get food and lodging in return for labour, who have nothing to do with their money unless it is to buy smart dresses and bonnets.

The great ambition of such servants generally is to copy the mistress; and if she dresses quietly they are pretty sure to follow her example. Among themselves they are all "young ladies." The kitchen-maid is called in the next house "the young lady who lives at Smith's," and the housemaid is "Miss Jones who is at Jackson's." If Mrs. Smith and Mrs. Jackson dress quietly, their young lady servants will do the same.

It must not be forgotten that finery is cheap, and that to dress quietly and well requires time and money. The late Dean of Gloucester used to say, "There should be nothing conspicuous about a lady; one should not notice the colour of her garments any more than that of the umbrella which she puts up when it is raining."

"Servants will never dress above the taste of their sweethearts, and men of their class like them to make a showy appearance. For one man who admires a quiet bonnet and sober-tinted gown, a dozen prefer a hat with a smart feather, and a dress of as many colours as the coat which Joseph put on to the disgust of his brethren.

General servants complain very much of want of liberty in choosing their "place of worship." "To tell a woman where she is to go to church is to interfere with the rights of a British subject," says a mistress. Nevertheless it is done again and again by mistresses; and bitter complaints have reached us on this subject from divers quarters. A respectable tradesman who visits fifty houses a day confirms this statement. He tells us that it is a constant source of bitterness among servants, especially among general servants. In large houses a pew is generally kept at some church for the servants; the late Lord Shaftesbury used to turn round in his parish church, and take a survey of his servants, who were arranged behind him. Such martial discipline is quite fair if the servants have warning before they are engaged; but general servants are not always told the religious tenets of the mistress. In fact, as the tradesman who has been already quoted said, "If mistresses were obliged to give characters to servants, as servants have to give to mistresses, many of the ladies would have to do their own work, for no amount of money would get them a servant."

CHAPTER IX.

SERVANTS VERSUS *MISTRESSES.*

WE have already mentioned a tradesman who has given us much information on the subject of servants. At his invitation a Commissioner went to meet some twenty servants, and have tea with them. The following is her account of the entertainment.

Mr. —— is head man in a grocer's shop, and calls for orders at some of the largest houses in the West End. His wife was formerly a servant, and he has many relations "in the domestic line of business." He is a Wesleyan, and teaches in a Wesleyan Sunday School. When our Commissioner arrived at his suburban villa, she was taken into a smart little sitting-room, full of chairs and sofas, with a large table in the centre. The table had a big Bible on it, also volumes of sermons, and a copy of "Pilgrim's Progress." This room opened into another apartment, and there the table was spread for tea. While waiting

8

for the arrival of the guests, the Commissioner asked Mr. —— to give her his opinion on the subject of "perquisites." He said that a friend of his, who is a butcher's assistant, had often talked to him about perquisites, and "in a well-ordered house" the scullery-maid has the bones, the kitchen-maid has the fat, and the cook has the dripping. Cooks or housekeepers receive presents from tradesmen at Christmas according to the amount of the year's purchases at the various shops, but butchers are their chief patrons. Butchers try to outbid one another with housekeepers and cooks in large London houses.

"It is in this way, you see," he said. "A butcher calls on a cook, and says, 'If you make your mistress give up her present butcher and come to my shop, I'll give you a commission on that, and discount every week while you trade with me.' Then the cook complains of the meat to the mistress, or she manages to cook it tough, and the mistress says to her, 'We shall have to change our butcher.' She pretends to be sorry, and recommends the man who has offered her a commission. Then the mistress changes the butcher, and if he writes to complain, the mistress says that the meat did not give satisfaction."

The Commissioner asked Mr. —— if cooks are in the habit of selling cooked meat, and told him about a house in Kensington where the mistress opened her back door one foggy morning, and had a basin thrust into her hands by some one who said, "Only three-penn'orth of beef to-day, and a little gravy."

"I don't know," he answered. "A friend of mine is coming here to-day who has been housekeeper in some of the largest London houses. She will tell you more than I can."

Then the guests began to arrive, and our Commissioner was introduced to ladies'-maids, housemaids, and cooks, also to three or four men-servants. A handsome young valet informed her that he had once thought of writing for the papers himself, but he had been told that the pay for such work was bad, and that writers had "no position." "I've heard my lady say, when she's been making up the list of people to have down at our country place, that, she must throw in a few writing folks to make it amusing. Writers don't bring much luggage, and by the look of their clothes I should say their purses are empty."

Our Commissioner asked this young man if it is true that servants take the rank of their master or mistress, namely, that the lady's-maid of a duchess has a higher place at the housekeeper's table than Abigail of a peeress.

"Certainly," he replied. "I've sat down to

dinner with fifty ladies'-maids before now, and it's been hard enough to remember their position. And if you dance with one after dinner because she's a bit good-looking, and forget another that's got a higher mistress, you may be sure you'll hear of it again from some one. It's like walking on the edge of a sword, visiting about in some of these big houses. The men are right enough, but the women stick up for their dignity. And if you happen to go to a place where the housekeeper and the butler don't hit it off, it's worse than living in a situation where the master and mistress aren't friendly. The master and mistress can get a divorce, but the butler and the cook can't. It looks like giving in for one to go away, so there they stay on quarrelling all the time, until the servants complain, or one poisons the mistress's mind against the other, or something else takes place to separate the unhappy parties."

The company then adjourned to tea. Our Commissioner was seated between the tradesman and a pretty little girl of sixteen. She asked the girl her name.

"Do you mean my real name, or the one I go by in the house?" the girl inquired.

"What do they call you in the house?"

"I go by the name of any favourite that's in—I mean any horse on which the men are betting"

Our Commissioner inquired if betting goes on to any great extent among female servants.

"Bless you," said the valet, "they're keener at it than the men. They don't gamble much, but they love betting."

"Why do they bet?"

"Because their lives are so dull. They must have some amusement," answered a lady's-maid. "I don't bet myself, but I know others that do. Sometimes they copy their master and mistress."

Then the tradesman, at our Commissioner's request, asked the company to suggest how "a better understanding can be brought about between servants and mistresses."

"In my opinion," said a rather solemn-looking man, "some one ought to write a book like 'Vice Versa,' and put the mistress in the servant's place."

"Or put the mistress behind the curtain of this room," suggested another, "and let her hear what we've got to say about mistresses."

"Mistresses have no consideration," the valet said, "nor have masters neither, unless they are aristocrats. I went to a house in —— Square, some years ago, and I came in the first afternoon through the front door. My master was in the hall, and he said, 'Will you have the goodness to come with me, and I'll show you *your* way in here?' He went to the area gate, and rung the bell. Says I, 'I *am* a gentleman, though I *am* a servant.' I walked in, packed my portmanteau, and left the house. Of course it isn't many can afford to be so independent, but I can, and it's a blessing."

"The airs some people give themselves!" remarked a smartly-dressed parlour-maid. "The other day a tradesman came to our house, and asked to see my mistress. I told her a gentleman wanted to see her. 'What do you mean,' said she, 'by calling a tradesman a gentleman?' 'Well, mam,' said I, 'I've been taught to call *every one* a gentleman, even a beggar. What else do you think I ought to call him?'"

"She wasn't much of a lady if she spoke to you like that," remarked another servant. "In good houses the master always calls his servants Mr. or Miss; he never thinks of doing anything else. It's only in second-class houses they treat servants without any consideration. But it isn't every one can get into a big house; some people must go into second-rate places, and then there is a great deal to put up with."

"My mistress said if I sauced her she'd send me away without a character," the parlour-maid continued. "I'll stay my year, although she's a Tartar. She makes me walk up in front of her to bed, and knock at her door so she may know at what time I get up in the morning. She sends me and the two others out sometimes, and then she and the master go down to the larder. They've nothing to do but worry us servants. If they'd keep to the parlour, and let us have the kitchen in peace, things would be easier to put up with."

"In my opinion," said a young woman, "the system of giving characters is at the root of the mischief, because it gives mistresses such a hold over servants. Times are bad, and work is scarce, so servants must look out, for without a character they can do nothing. If a mistress wishes to spite a girl she can do it. Besides now it's always 'personal' characters that are wanted, and mistresses get confabulating over servants instead of writing down what they have to say for and against them on paper. They want to know when you were born, and they'd like you to give them a burial certificate. It's that 'no character' business that keeps servants so humble with mistresses. I don't see what can be done, but I sometimes think that the system of giving characters should be changed by Act of Parliament."

"If so," remarked the valet, "it would have to be done by the Upper House. It's only the aristocracy who treat servants properly. I tried one situation out of aristocratic circles, and that was where the man showed me his area gate. The aristocracy know how to behave to a gentleman, even if he happens to be a servant."

"Well, I've been both a servant and a mistress," remarked a middle-aged woman. "I began as kitchen-maid, and I worked up to my last place, where I was housekeeper. I left because, although I pleased the master, I couldn't get on with the mistress. I believe servants like to be under a housekeeper better than under a lady, for housekeepers have been servants themselves, and know how to show consideration. I always let a servant see the kitchen and her sleeping accommodation before I engaged her, and I went more by her looks than her character. The best girl I ever had came to me with this letter:—'Jane —— has been with me one year, and went away to nurse her mother.' I think the system of letting a cook engage her own kitchen-maids and scullery-maids excellent, and the housemaid should engage her own servants too, also the head nurse her nursery-maids. Then there is order in the house, and without order every one becomes miserable. I gave my scullery-maid from £10 to £12 a year, and my kitchen maids from £16 to £18 a year, with their proper perquisites. Three meat meals a day was my rule for everybody; I was not extravagant, and I was not stingy. Nothing was wasted, for all the scraps went to make soup for beggars. Every servant had $\frac{1}{4}$lb. tea, $\frac{1}{2}$lb. butter, and $\frac{3}{4}$lb. sugar every week. Besides, I let the servants under me have a fixed time free each day. That's a thing ladies seldom think of doing. A servant likes to know how much time is her own, and to do what she pleases then without interference. Ladies seem to think that they buy servants body and soul for so much a year, and forget that a servant ought to be her own mistress for some part of the day, as well as every other Sunday."

"How many women servants were there in your last place?" inquired the Commissioner.

"Well, there was me, the cook, two kitchen-maids, a scullery-maid, three housemaids, a school-room maid, and a lady's-maid, that's nine. Oh no, there were ten of us; I quite forgot the governess."

We shall next look at the question from the other side: Mistresses *versus* Servants.

CHAPTER X.

MISTRESSES VERSUS *SERVANTS.*

HAVING read "Servants *versus* Mistresses" in our last issue, Lady Florence ——, who is a constant reader of THE BRITISH WEEKLY, invited a Commissioner to meet half-a-dozen mistresses at her house, in order that the Commissioner might hear what ladies have to say about servants. Lady Florence made what is called "a love marriage," namely, a matrimonial alliance in which money was a secondary consideration. The result is three children, a small house, and a limited income, all of which things she "puts up with." But she groans over her servants.

"My dear! *have* you found a parlour-maid yet?" she inquired, as one of the half-dozen ladies was announced by her own neat little maid-servant.

The lady shook her head, and gave a graphic account of her difficulties.

"London servants," she said, "will starve in the streets sooner than go to service. The clergyman's wife in our parish tells me that the mothers foolishly take the part of the girls, and that nothing can be done to put sense into them. Her husband is going to preach a sermon on the subject."

"I wonder what he will take for his text!" exclaimed Lady Florence. "My cook is dreadfully untidy, and I cannot persuade her to look after her clothes. Only think, then, what my feelings were last Sunday week! A foolish young curate walked into the pulpit, and preached on the text, 'Consider the lilies of the field.' You know how it goes on. My cook was there, of course; and the next morning when I tried to explain away all that the foolish young man had said in the pulpit, she answered, 'It isn't every one that thinks so much of dress as your ladyship.'"

"I do not know what will become of servants," sighed another lady. "I was actually told the other day by a housemaid who applied for my place, 'I'm not particular, mam, but I *must* have scented soap to wash with, and I can only eat delicate puddings.'"

"Servants used to be so different!" remarked another lady. "My husband's old nurse comes every year to visit us. She has a pension, and travels about to see her 'young ladies and gentlemen,' as she calls them still, although they are all married. But *then* servants had no education. She wrote to say, after she left us, that she had my youngest boy 'in her mind's high.' I believe that the difficulties mistresses have to put up with now are the result of over-education among servants. What do *you* think?" she inquired of our Commissioner.

The Commissioner said that it was not the business of people who write for the press to form opinions on any subject, and that she had merely come there to report the opinions of half-a dozen mistresses on the subject of maid-servants. But she quoted as an example of "over-education" a parlour-maid who is in the family of a well-known M.P. This woman told our Commissioner that she enjoys her position as parlour-maid because it gives her an opportunity of hearing what is going on in politics. "I look forward to *our* political dinner-parties," she said, "and I enjoy the waiting, for then I hear all that politicians are thinking and doing. I make my hands and feet do the mechanical work, and I listen to the conversation."

She went away to be married two years ago, but her husband died about a year after her marriage, and then she begged the wife of the M.P. to take her back again. She has the greatest respect for her master, and admiration for her mistress. Speaking of the former, she said, "He is that *h*onest, he is only fit to be a Prime Minister;" and of the latter, "She can hold her own with him, although he is a Member of Parliament."

"Servants are so suspicious," said another mistress. "It does not matter how kind you are to them, how much you put yourself about, they look upon you as their natural enemy. I believe it has always been the same from the beginning, and will remain so to the end, except in exceptional cases. It comes from our 'dual' establishments, I mean two families in one house, with no go-between but the children. And the children soon cease to be a 'go-between,' for it does not do to let boys be intimate with maid-servants."

"Of course," said Lady Florence, "it would be easy to place servants on quite a different footing in the house if it were not for the young men. The great ambition of a woman servant is to marry a gentleman. She does not think, poor thing, of all she will have to bear from him and his relations. I know a lady's-maid who married the son of a baronet, and she came to consult me the other day about her little boy. 'I don't know how it is,' she said, 'but I can't get him to talk like a gentleman. He uses queer words, and drops his *h*'s, and that makes his father angry. His father seems quite ashamed of him. I can put up with slights from my husband's relations myself, but I can't bear to see my children slighted.'"

A long conversation then took place about young men who fall in love with servants, and our Commissioner was asked to give her opinion. She could only quote her own father, who always showed to his women-servants the same courtesy that he showed to visitors of their sex, who bowed to them out of doors, and taught his sons to behave as he did.

"My servants always come upstairs on Christmas Day (unless it is Sunday) to play games with the children," said a lady, "and on New Year's Day my children go downstairs to tea in the kitchen. But it is always done by written invitation: the children write to the servants and the servants write to the children."

"That does not remove the difficulty of the two families," remarked the lady who had previously said that servants are "so suspicious." "Once a day all the inhabitants of the house meet at prayers, and then they separate for the day. One family lives upstairs, and the other downstairs; there is no place where they come together except the nursery."

"I see no help for that," said Lady Florence. "All are equal when they die, but here there must be social distinctions. I remember when my grandmother was buried in the family vault, and the water got into it, an old servant said, 'To think that her ladyship, who was so much better off than us when she was alive, is so much worse off when she is buried! We *do* get dry graves, at any rate.'"

"Well, I think that servants are very much to be envied," said another mistress. "They have comfortable homes, good food, kind treatment, no responsibilities, and money enough to be independent in their old age. In return for all this we have a right to expect from them gratitude, at any rate. Yet they are the most ungrateful race under the face of the sun, and the most deceitful. What do *you* think, Lady Florence?"

"Oh, don't ask me!" groaned Lady Florence. "My present cook is dirty, and my last cook was impertinent. The last one always quoted her previous mistress, and used to say, 'Mrs. —— did this, or that; but then she *was* a lady.' At last I had to turn her out of the house, with a month's wages, at a moment's notice. She refused to go, because I am a widow; and when I told her that I should send for my friend Mr. ——, who lives close by, to make her go away, she said, 'Your friend! I came up with him in a third-class carriage from the City last week. A nice sort of friend *he* is, to travel in a third-class carriage!' Of course she was tipsy, but all London cooks seem given to drinking."

"If things go on like this we shall soon have to do the work ourselves, for good servants are rare, and bad servants are such a nuisance," said a lady. "'The levelling spirit of the age,' my husband calls it. I hope before long we shall see the work done by machinery, for in London young women will even go into the Salvation Army sooner than become servants."

"There are *some* Christian servants left," observed another lady—"young women who are content with the position in which it has pleased God to place them. Their number is few, I admit; but some few remember the text: 'Servants, be obedient to them that are your masters according to the flesh, with fear and trembling, in singleness of your heart as unto Christ.' Such servants find good mistresses, for the Bible commands, in more than seven hundred places, that servants should be treated with love and kindness. When servants are unmannerly and impudent, it cannot be expected that they should find sympathetic mistresses; but if they study their employers, their employers will study them—at least, that is *my* experience."

"How to treat women-servants is a problem," sighed Lady Florence. "They are much more difficult to deal with than men-servants."

"The problem to me has always been how men can bear to be waited upon by women," remarked our Commissioner. "I have not the smallest compunction about men-servants; I do not care how often I send them up and downstairs, or how much I make them fetch and carry; they are strong, and if they like the position of menials it is not my business. But when I see a parlour-maid waiting on half-a-dozen men, walking about the room with a pale face, dragging herself from seat to seat, looking ill, sometimes half-fainting, I always wonder how the men can enjoy their dinner. Some men cannot bear it, and will not be waited upon at all if they cannot afford to keep a man-servant. But most men never seem to see anything but the *ménu*, or to think of any one but the cook."

"I heard a man say to his wife, not long ago, 'I will not let you dismiss Mrs. ——' (the cook). 'I could get another wife, but I could not replace Mrs. ——. So you must put up with her,'" laughed a mistress. "Some of the happiest marriages I have known have been between masters and cooks," she continued ; "I intend all of my daughters to learn cooking."

The conversation then turned on the subject of men-servants, and Lady Florence related an anecdote about a footman who was in the service of Mr. Studd, the father of the famous cricketers. Some of the ladies thought the anecdote frivolous; and our Commissioner wished them good-bye, as we have nothing to do with men-servants in these articles.

CHAPTER XI.

REGISTRY OFFICES.

WE are indebted to Mr. Coote, Secretary of the National Vigilance Association, for the information we are able to give on the subject of Registry Offices. Mr. Coote has throughout our inquiry done all that he can to assist our Commissioners. In this he has acted very differently to some of the religious and philanthropic societies and associations with which our Commissioners have come in contact. "What is the use of writing on such subjects?" they were asked again and again. Sometimes doors were slammed in their faces, sometimes they were kept waiting for hours, sometimes it was said "the press is so conceited."

The National Vigilance Association has removed to 267, Strand, and there its secretary may be found at work all day, and sometimes all night. Servants' Registry Offices, he says, may be divided into three classes: 1. Those which take fees from both servant and mistress; 2. Free registries, where the mistress pays the fee and the servant pays nothing, or something after she has entered into the situation; 3. Registries for foreign servants. At many of these registries girls are provided with lodgings until they obtain situations, and here they sleep five or six in a room, two or three in a bed, for sixpence a night.

Of course some of these registries are respectable places, but many are very pernicious, and not a few are wholly bad. Registries are commercially difficult. If the proprietor is anxious to safeguard servants, his business generally comes to nothing. Those registries which are conducted on the merchandise principle, where the interest of the proprietor begins and ends with the fee, and girls are bundled off to situations without inquiries as to where they are going, or who is to be their mistress, will bring in money; but registries conducted on philanthropic principles seldom pay, and certainly do not make much profit.

Girls cannot be too often warned against the advertisements of registries which offer situations with high wages and little work. These are generally held by scamps, who advertise freely to attract customers, and then clear off, sometimes to begin again in a new place, with a new name. One such man, who had previously been a police-detective, carried on a notorious business for swindling servants. His office was closed by the police. He changed his name and began again. He even went to the Vigilance Association, and offered to go on their committee, saying that his experience as a detective would be useful to the Association. One of his tricks was to keep a dozen good-looking girls on the premises to see mistresses. An engagement with one of these girls was made in his office by the mistress, and the fee was paid. But the girl did not enter the situation. Some excuse was made, and when the mistress reclaimed the fee, he said it was not his fault that the girl would not keep to the engagement. Many such scamps start registry offices for servants; in fact, the Vigilance Society has a book filled in with the names of "suspected" registries. These cannot be published, but we shall give at the close of this article the names of the safest and the best metropolitan registries. From "suspected registries" girls are often sent into bad houses. Dozens of complaints have been brought to the Vigilance Association about situations entered into by girls in ignorance of the character of the mistress. One case the Association has taken up, that of a girl who was charged by her mistress with stealing a pair of boots. It was discovered that the girl was innocent, and that the charge had been brought to punish her because she would not copy the evil habits of her mistress. Servants should be on their guard against entering any house connected with a registry office unless they have taken pains to know the character of the place. Sometimes the proprietors of such houses run up bills the servants cannot pay, and then turn them out late at night to shift for themselves, detaining their boxes. The greatest number of frauds take place in foreign registries. Some of these are carried on by foreigners, and some by English people. They bring girls over from the Continent, or send English girls to European cities. Some have agents in Germany, whose business it is to advertise English situations in glowing colours, promising at the same time high wages and passage money. When girls apply to the agents they are told that an agreement must be signed, and then they can go at once to England. Their boxes are sent by a different route, arriving in London before the girls themselves. These boxes contain all their worldly goods, sometimes clothes to the amount of £15 and £20. When the girls reach the London registries, the proprietor asks for their passage-money, and if they wish to go away, saying that according to the agreement there is nothing to pay for the journey, he takes advantage of the fact that they cannot speak English. Eighty per cent. of the girls give in to him, and enter the house attached to the registry. He then runs them up a bill for board and lodging. Bit by bit the girls sell all their clothing, and then in despair they add to the large number of foreign prostitutes.

The following case was taken into court by Mr. Coote, and the plaintiff received £15 damages.

Maria Geiger, native of Stuttgart, Germany, brought an action against the keeper of a registry office and home for servants, for the delivery up of her box of wearing apparel, and for damages for detaining the same, and for breach of contract in refusing to obtain her a situation.

Plaintiff said, "Before coming to England I lived with my father and mother at Stuttgart, and while there saw an advertisement in a Stuttgart paper for German girls to go to England for domestic situations. I went to the office advertised, and saw Pfeiffer (who was admitted to be the defendant's agent). He told me to send my box on to England, and gave me the defendant's address to put on it. He also gave me a card with the defendant's name and address on it, on which he was described as 'Late of the Criminal Investigation Department, Great Scotland Yard, S.W., and also Official Interpreter of the Criminal Police, 2, Official Law Courts, London.' Pfeiffer told me I could have a place from defendant if I came to England. He told me to send my box over in advance, but that I should not have to pay for it. He advanced me forty marks for my journey. I went to the defendant's house the day after I came to London, but he was out. The next day I saw him, and he asked me if I was Maria Geiger, and whether I had my certificates. He spoke to me in a rude manner, and said he would not give me a place. I said again, 'Do give me a place.' He said, 'No, I won't;' and then asked me to refund him 50*s*. He fixed the sum of 10*s*. for the carriage of my box, and 40*s*. for my journey. He has not found me a place. I was without a place some weeks, when I got one from Gordon House (a German Home). I am not paid any money in my place; I only accepted it because I had no clothing or money. I saw my box at defendant's house. It is worth from £15 to £20. I have spent £5 for board and lodging, and have borrowed £1 to buy clothing.

Cross-examined by Mr. Browning, she said: "I arrived in London Tuesday, 26th October. The reason I did not go straight to defendant was because I was warned on board the steamer that many girls were decoyed to London and got into bad places. A gentleman on board the steamer advised me to stay at the Essex Hotel, Shoreditch, while I made inquiries. He came the next day, and took me to the defendant's. He did so again the following day. On the second day the defendant called me all sorts of bad names, and used bad language. I told him I was afraid, and therefore did not go straight to him. He said, 'I will send you back at once; as to the box, you can pledge your watch and earrings to pay.' I then went straight to the German Consulate, where I was given the address of the German Home and the National Vigilance Association."

With regard to foreign situations, an English mother writes as follows to Mr. Coote :—

"Some weeks back a young friend of mine, who is an orphan, came to stay at my house while seeking a situation. She answered an advertisement inserted by a foreign agency office, the manager of which, after some correspondence, instructed her to apply for a situation at Vienna, requesting her to forward her photograph. She did so, and later on received a note telling her she was engaged to go to Vienna, and must call at the office the Monday following. As she was an inexperienced country girl, I thought it better to go with her, and found, to my surprise, that she was expected to travel on the following Saturday, without giving references and knowing the address of the lady to whom she was going, the business having been entirely arranged between the agent abroad and the agent here. She was instructed as to her journey, and was told to have her boxes addressed with the name of the foreign agent. Two other girls were to travel with her to the same destination. I set inquiries on foot, which resulted in the girls being saved from a fate worse than death, and I want through you to impress upon all girls to accept no situation abroad through any agency whatever, however apparently straightforward its business transactions may be, unless they have name and address of the lady abroad who engages them, with references to the English Consul and the Chaplain of the Embassy, and time to verify such references."

The following is a list of trustworthy metropolitan registries for servants:—

WEST.—Miss Bath, 69 Norfolk Terrace, Notting Hill; Dudley Stuart Registry, 8, Star Street, Edgware Road; Mrs. Faircloth, 106, Regent Street; The Misses Faithful, 136, Regent Street; Female Servants' Home Society, 205, Great Portland Place; Female Servants' Home Society, 21, Nutford Place, Edgware Road; M. Fitch, 296, King Street West, Hammersmith; Mrs. Foley (Roman Catholic), 26, King Street, Portman Square; Mrs. Hay, 52, Regent Street; Mrs. Heeld, 38, Westbourne Grove, Bayswater; Miss Hoyt (Roman Catholic), 47, South Street, Park Lane; Mrs. Hunt, 32, Duke Street, Manchester Square; Miss Maulden, 153, Church Street, Paddington Green; Mrs. Norman, 77, Great Portland Street; Mrs. Perry, 9, George Street, Portman Square; Servants' Registry, Soho Bazaar, 77, Oxford Street; Soho Club and Home, 59, Greek Street, Soho Square.

S.W.—Mrs. Cooke, 64, Fulham Road; Elm Park Registry, 319, Fulham Road; Miss Freeman, 162, Warwick Street; Mrs. Hawley, 159, Sloane Street; Mrs. Holton, 2, Dartrey Road, King's Road; Mrs. Lord, 12, Gloucester Road, South Kensington; Miss Lovejoy, 32, Sydney Street, Chelsea; Working Women's Home and Registry, 53, Horseferry Road, Westminster; Mrs. Turner, 361, Clapham Road; Mrs. Curtis, 322A, Brixton Road.

W.C.—Foreign Women Servants' Institute, 36, Hart Street, Bloomsbury; Miss M. M. Moran, 29, Queen Square, Bloomsbury.

N.W.—Mrs. George, 42, Camden Road.

NORTH.—Mrs. Hunter, 517, Holloway Road; Mrs. Goddard, 228, Liverpool Road, Islington; Miss Franks, 252, Upper Street, Highbury; Mrs. Smith, 138, Upper Street, Islington.

EAST.—Mrs. Burd, 386, Commercial Road; Mrs. Winter, 96, Mile End Road.

Also the offices connected with M.A.B.Y.S. (Metropolitan Association for Befriending Young Servants); Young Women's Christian Association, and Girls' Friendly Society.

CHAPTER XII.

FOREIGN SERVANTS.

"WHAT can be done to stop the immigration of girls from Germany into England?"

This question was put by a Commissioner to the German Consul at his office in Finsbury Circus. Captain von Roeder pointed to the piles of letters on his table, and said:

"A German girl is a free agent. We cannot prevent her from leaving Germany; all we can do is to warn her against coming to London. I have heart-rending cases here every week, and I feel very helpless. But things are much better than they used to be. With the help of Mr. Coote and others, I have been able to expose many of the fraudulent agencies. Directly I hear of a place that employs bad agents over in Germany, I communicate with the German police. It is very difficult to catch these agents, for they are so cunning, but we have managed to put a stop to most of them, and the box-trick is nearly played out. Still the girls *will* come. They hear of the high wages over here, and they think if once they set foot in London they will make their fortune. They forget that the competition is greater here than in our country, and that things are more expensive. We do all we can to warn them against coming. We write in the German newspapers, and we print notices. But the girls come nevertheless, and the result is a terrible amount of suffering."

Captain von Roeder then showed our Commissioner a letter he had received that morning from a German girl in a lunatic asylum.

"Her brain would not stand all the trouble she was obliged to go through, and now she writes me these letters," he said. "German girls go mad over here, and many find their way to the workhouse. I do my best, but it is a very difficult business."

As our Commissioner left the office she passed through a crowd of poor foreigners who were waiting to see the Consul. One poor man was crying bitterly over his papers. Another was wringing his hands, and asking in broken English what he was to do, for he had not a penny left, and he could not find employment. Captain von Roeder certainly has a painful and difficult task, and only those who have witnessed his patient kindness know how to appreciate him.

The next visit was to Gordon House, 8, Endsleigh Gardens, N.W., the well-known home for foreign servants and governesses. Miss Seebo, the Superintendent, was away. The lady taking her place brought two girls under our Commissioner's notice. The one was an Austrian, the other a Roumanian. They had been two months in London, and they were literally starving. Neither of them could speak a word of English. The Austrian was a fair girl of about twenty, the Roumanian had dark eyes and hair, and an eager little face. They had been to the German Consul, the Russian Consul, and the Austrian Consul; and they were then on their way to see what Prince Ghika could do to help them.

The Austrian girl had no parents; she wanted to go to Canada, where she has a sister. In her hand she held a dirty bit of newspaper, which enclosed her sister's photograph and address. Her idea was that if she came to London she could easily earn enough money to get on to Canada. She arrived with 30*s.*, and was taken from the ship to a lodging near the docks. While there she met a German woman who had known her parents, and this woman took compassion on her forlorn condition. With this woman she had lived ever since her 30*s*. were exhausted. She had sold all her clothes, everything but the few rags she had on, before she came to Gordon House. Her feet were bleeding, and she was so weak that she found it difficult to stand upright. She was rather pretty, and had come from the tradesmen's class in Vienna. During her two months in England she had had two or three situations among people near the docks, but she had been turned away because she was slow in picking up English.

The Roumanian was also on her way to America. She brought two pounds to London, and meant to make enough here to pay for her passage. But the two pounds were spent while she was in lodgings. All her clothes and her box had been sold, and she must have drifted into the streets or the workhouse if the Austrian girl had not met her, and taken her to the room of the German woman. She had, also, held several small situations, and had worked for two days in a factory ; but from all these places she had been turned away because she could not speak English.

It was arranged that our Commissioner should accompany the Superintendent to the house of the woman with whom the girls were lodging, in order to see if their story could be corroborated. But it was difficult to discover the situation of this house, for all the girls could say was that it lay in the Jews' Quarter, 50, Siegel Street, and that it was four hours away from Endsleigh Gardens.

Meanwhile the Superintendent brought some dinner. But although they had not eaten anything that day they declined the food, saying that they must not eat the meat, as it had not been killed in Jewish fashion.

"I have nothing but my religion left," the Austrian said, with tears in her blue eyes. "I would rather starve than do anything against my religion."

After they had had some coffee our Commissioner took them to Aldgate, and set out from thence to find "the Jews' Quarter." When they saw the Whitechapel Church they were delighted. "We make our way from that," they said (in German). "It is the only thing that looks like home here in London."

After passing through innumerable back streets they stopped at "Grey Eagle Street," which they had written "Siegel Street." Here our Commissioner found their hostess in one of the smallest but cleanest rooms she has ever seen in Whitechapel. The woman is called "Frau

Friedmanlieber." She cannot speak English, She explained that the girls were "green," and that she kept them there for fear that they should get into trouble. But her husband has lost his work, and now they are all starving. She had two little children, and it was quite impossible for her to feed the girls, although they might lie on the floor. Every other night, she explained, her husband lay on the floor and let one of the girls share her bed, but he could not do that always. The girls did their best to find work, but no one wanted them—there were already too many English girls in England—and they must go into the workhouse.

It ended in taking the girls to the Jewish Board of Guardians, where a handsome dark-haired man promised to look after them. He was especially pleased to hear that the Austrian girl had refused to eat a Christian dinner, and told our Commissioner to send him all similar cases that came under her notice.

We have given the histories of these girls at some length, because they are very typical of the stories we hear about German servants. No other country deluges us with young women like Germany. It is a serious fact that German girls add largely to the class of fallen women in London. When a German girl loses her self-respect she sinks much lower than a French girl, or an English girl, and her case is more hopeless. Germans are tempted over here by the high wages of English servants. A girl arrived lately in London who had been earning only £5 a year in Germany. She wanted to go to Liverpool Street, but said "Liverpool," so she was sent on there by the guard. The German Consul in Liverpool returned her to the German Consul in London, and he forwarded her to Gordon House.

Board and lodging can be had at Gordon House for 4*s.* 6*d.* a week, including breakfast, dinner, and tea. A bed costs 2*s.* 6*d.* per week, and a separate cubicle can be had for 4*s.* per week. Separate meals cost as follows: Breakfast 2*d.*, dinner 6½*d.*, tea 2½*d.*, supper 1½*d.* This Home is a great boon to foreign servants, and mistresses who dismiss foreign girls ought to give them this address, instead of turning them out into the streets, as is only too often done at the shortest possible notice.

We heard of a poor French *bonne* lately who was rescued by a gentleman from a crowd of boys near Westminster. She wanted to find Victoria Station, and had lost her way, to the great amusement of the London urchins. The poor thing was talking fast in her native language, and struggling to escape from her tormentors.

She had been turned away from her situation, and was on her way to Paris.

Foreign servants often find it difficult to get on with English servants, and the result is quarrels that end in the foreigner being dismissed. They receive, as a rule, less wages than the English, and they do not want "perquisites." They work much harder than the English. These things are especially true of Germans, and the English servants resent their "ways," including their dirty habits. There is no doubt that foreign servants are less "up to the mark" than English servants; they are apt to be slovenly and untidy. They are also very touchy, and cry over trifles which English girls laugh at. Added to these things they have many foreign habits which our countrywomen think uncanny, such as making mysterious potions when they are ill, collecting herbs, and cooking sundry dishes, into which they introduce (so the English servants persist) frogs and slugs, without which they could not live away from their own country.

Mistresses who wish to keep foreign servants should try to get two or three from the same country. Then things go on smoothly, and the foreigners do not grow homesick.

Captain von Roeder speaks very highly of the Travellers' Aid Society (which we have already mentioned) and the other societies who meet foreign girls when they arrive in England. Sharpers are always on the look-out for such victims, and a great deal of mischief is done under the pretence of showing kindness. Thus Germans and French people meet their country-women at the landing-places, and take them to bad lodging-houses. Case after case has come under our notice in which the girl has been robbed of her clothes and her box by sharpers who offered to help her. We cannot say if English girls are equally credulous, but German girls seem to lend an ear to the first person who offers them assistance.

Thus we heard of a German girl the other day who arrived in London with a chest of drawers that contained all her property. She had come over in the steerage, and was on her way to a situation in Woolwich. When she arrived in London no one came to meet her. She had no idea how to find the train, and was quite overcome when she heard that very few trains go on Sunday to Woolwich. A first-class passenger, a young Englishman, who had made her acquaintance on the boat, asked her to spend the day with him, offering to show her "the sights of London." She drove off with him to his lodgings, with the chest of drawers on the top of the cab, not knowing where he lived or anything about him.

Such are the girls who make Captain von Roeder shake his head and groan over his letters. When they get into trouble their first thought is, "I must go to the German Consul."

He tries to harden his heart, but we venture to say that no German girl wants help if Captain von Roeder is able to give it.

CHAPTER XIII.

LETTERS FROM SERVANTS.

READERS will find that each of these letters embodies at least one grievance. We have chosen them out of a varied correspondence, which has come to us in most instances carefully sealed, with "Private" or "Personal" written on the envelope. The writers have all been visited, and our Commissioners can vouch for the truth of the statements. Two or three of the letters reached us through a Bible Christian, a young man who is now studying for the ministry, and who takes a great interest in servants. This young man began life in a butcher's shop. He used to rise at four o'clock every morning while he worked as a butcher, and study until he went to his duties at seven. He returned home at four in the afternoon, washed himself, and studied on until twelve at night. While he was in the butcher's establishment he became acquainted with many servants. He wrote to THE BRITISH

WEEKLY offering information, and when he came to London, a few weeks ago, from the Cumberland village where he preaches to the miners, he set to work among his former acquaintances, asking them to take this opportunity of stating their grievances in the columns of THE BRITISH WEEKLY. He found no difficulty in collecting the letters, but was obliged to promise that he would keep the names of the writers secret. Several things have struck us while perusing this correspondence: (1) The greatest objection servants have to domestic service is "loss of independence." (2) Sitting in dark London kitchens with large fires and constant gas makes servants feel their life a burden, and envy their masters and mistresses (3) "Dressing-time," or whatever else servants like to call it, should be extended, and during those hours they ought not to be interfered with under any pretence. (4) Fresh air and sunshine being necessary to health, servants should be allowed much more out-door exercise than they get at present. (5) Hotel servants ought to be recognised as respectable members of society, and not tabooed in private houses, as is the case at present.

A TRADESMAN'S SERVANT.

DEAR COMMISSIONER,—I came to London in 1874. A lady (?), who married from the neighbourhood of my home, promised if I would go to London with her I should be treated as one of the family. That promise shared the same fate as the much-spoken-about pie-crust. I found I had come to a large tradesman's establishment. The household numbered twenty-nine, including the servants, which were four in number. Sixteen men slept in the house. As I had no friends in London, I had to make the best of it. Our hours were from six till ten, during which time we were always on the go. My duties were those of housemaid, for which I was paid the handsome sum of six pounds a year. I was forbidden to go out, although I was eighteen years of age. During the time I was always found fault with. I was once stopped on my way out by a person "dressed in a little brief authority," and asked whether an article I had on did not belong to my mistress. Masters and mistresses of the tradesman type forget that servants are human beings like themselves, and in fact have none of the true gentleman or lady about them. Servants might often ask, "Is thy servant a dog?" This state of things will not last for ever, and we servants are grateful to you and to Mr. Editor for your painstaking efforts.

HOPEFUL.

A TRADESMAN'S SERVANT.

MADAM,—Will you let an outraged father tell you his feelings about servants in tradesmen's houses? because if you do very likely many girls may be benefited. My daughter's former mistress (I took her away directly I knew, of course, and now she is in a respectable situation) is the wife of a man who keeps a shop. He leaves home early and comes back late, so his wife knows he will be away all day. Well, she used to take my girl out with her after breakfast and stop at all the public-houses. Sometimes she could not walk home straight, and then she would send my girl after that to a public-house for spirits. Before her husband comes in she puts her head in a basin of cold water, and sometimes she says she feels faint, and there is such goings on for him not to smell the drink, which he seems not to have done till I took my daughter away on account of his wife's habits. Then the mistress said it was all a lie, and wouldn't give her a character, though I proved my girl had been sent to the public-houses, which are no fit place for a young woman.

A BENEFACTOR OF "THE BRITISH WEEKLY."

A KITCHEN-MAID NEAR LANCASTER GATE.

DEAR LADY,—This is my experience in a house near Lancaster Gate: I came from the country to London about three years ago, and my first situation as kitchen-maid was near Lancaster Gate, W. This was obtained by applying at a registry office in the vicinity. Twelve servants were kept, both sexes being equal in number. As may be imagined, I found a great change from the country. I soon found out the house was a very gay one. I was engaged by the housekeeper, to whom the mistress sent me. I soon found I had eleven mistresses and masters, and did not know which to please. When I left I was refused a good character because I did not obey the housemaid. My employers indulged in dinner-parties, lawn-tennis, billiards, etc.; hence we had to work harder on Sunday than on week-days. The family used to go to horse-races, taking the men-servants with them, and coming home often "over the way." All the talk at table (among the servants) was about the racing, betting, etc.; sporting papers, books, etc., lying all around the room. I was called by the name of one of the favourite horses, "Bendigo." The betting usually took the form of sweepstakes. The cook, who came from the country a "nice, quiet girl," learnt betting here, and once got thirty shillings while I lived with her. She has since been married to a man who does nothing else but bet on races, games, matches, etc. Often we could not go out for weeks together. The mistress, as may be imagined, did not care anything about the morals of her servants. If the majority of the servants took a dislike to a girl she was doomed. Having now left, we may well pray, "From such mistresses, situations, and fellow-servants, good Lord, deliver us."

ALPHA.

A COOK IN HOSPITAL.

LADY COMMISSIONER,—You promised not to tell my name, and I write you these few lines remembering your promise, because I might never get another place if my mistress got ear I had been complaining. There is ten in family, and only two of us servants to do the work. I had my knee bad this last six months, and often when I have been obliged to scrub my kitchen I've got up and down screaming, because my knee was so stiff, and the mistress said it was rheumatics. We had oilcloth over the kitchen-floor, and that draws in the water, the doctor says, for when the oilcloth was took up when he come to visit me we found three oilcloths, one on the top of another, and underneath pools of water in the holes of the bricks, what the doctor said the oilcloths had sucked in. My mistress was very much taken back by what the medical gentleman said about the oilcloths, and she paid my cab, and she's been to see me once, so has my mother, who is a widow in poor circumstances. Now, dear lady, for God's sake don't tell any one my name, and if my mistress sees this letter in your paper, say it doesn't come from me, dear lady; and God bless you in your work for us poor servants.

Your obedient servant,

—— ——

A West End Housemaid.

Madam,—I have been in London about nine years, during which time I have been in three different situations as housemaid. I may therefore be allowed to say a few words about servants and mistresses. I was in my first place two months. The reason I left was because I had to do the washing, which I was told I had not to do when I was engaged. That was "too much of a good thing." My second mistress and master were Catholics, and I lived with them five years. Sunday afternoon and evening were devoted to parties and card-playing. The work was very hard. The family number nine, and two servants had to do the work, including dinner-parties. There should not have been less than four. Wages were very low, especially considering the work we had to do. My only reason for leaving was that the work injured my health. I have been in my present place three years. The work is not so hard as in my last place, but it is bad enough. What is worse than the work is the whims of my mistress. I am a Dissenter, but am supposed to go to the Established Church as they do. I can scarcely ever get out for myself, but I must go whenever they choose to send me; if I am busy or ill it makes no difference. She is neither willing for me to go to see my friends nor for them to come to see me. Many pounds are spent on parties, but if the servants have more butter than is thought proper there is a great fuss. All this comes of living beyond means, and trying to keep up appearances as if they were as well off as their neighbours. Servants are treated more as slaves than free persons. If my mistress knew I wrote this I should be discharged at once, so, madam, I trust you will keep my name secret.

CLEOPATRA.

P.S.—If one's brother comes on a visit he is reckoned as a burglar.—C.

A GENERAL SERVANT.

DEAR COMMISSIONER,—Will you tell the servants to ask if a gas-stove is kept before they take a situation, for them stoves is the cruellest things in the winter? My mistress makes me turn off the gas after seven o'clock, and I sit shivering till prayer-time, when I go to bed with cold feet, and I cry sometimes becos I can't well help myself. There is no hot water, becos my mistress has a coal fire in the parlour what she boils a kettle on for the hot water when she goes to bed. Them gas-stoves is handy in the morning, but my mistress turns the gas off herself if I forget to do it after I've washed up, and them is the cruellest things for us poor servants.

Your dutiful

—— ——

A CHAMBERMAID IN THE —— HOTEL.

DEAR MADAM,—I have been in my present place five years, and before then I was in another hotel three years, so I can speak for public service, which is very different to private service, and much better to my mind.

I had twenty-five rooms to do in the other place, but here I have only thirteen. I get £17 a year, which is the wages, I think, everywhere for chambermaids. Last year I made over £25 by "tips," and another girl got £30. I don't know how she did it, for she is in the back wing, but she is a bit flighty. I know chambermaids that make more than that, but our hotel is very select, and since I've been here only one girl has been turned away for being flighty. Our head waiter made £200 in quite a little time, and he told me he'd heard of a head waiter that had made £400 in one year, and that had refused the place of manager, because he could make more as he is by his waiting. Well, we are fifteen chambermaids, and we do the rooms between us. All our work is done by three in the afternoon, and then we dress, and we have tea at five, after which we light up, and then we've nothing to do but to mind our bells till we do the rooms at eight o'clock. We go to bed at ten, all but two of us, who is up till twelve. Our food is beautiful, because we have the leavings from the table-dote—lobster salad and all. We have great fun among us servants, and we bet on the steeple-races; that is, we did it once, but the manager got wind of it, and now we've no betting among us women servants. I know the public service has a bad name, but that is because some hotels keep fast girls to bring gentlemen about the place, and in a select hotel like ours the housekeeper would send us away if we were flighty. The housekeeper is very strict, but she don't interfere when us leave work at three o'clock, and she gives us our days out as it comes convenient. I say, "Give a dog a bad name and hang him," and so it is with the public service.

A Contented Chambermaid.

A SUBURBAN SERVANT.

MADAM,—My opinion is ladies have not enough work themselves, and that is why they like to call us servants lazy. My mistress does fancy needlework, and yet she can't let me have time to mend my own stockings. If I sit down a minute she rings the bell or calls out above the kitchen steps, and last week I caught her at a mean trick, for I was watching her over the banisters, and I saw her upset the visiting-cards on the hall-table *on purpose.* Then she rang the bell, and told me to go and put the cards straight. And again, she was angry with me because I opened the door to a visitor before she had time to settle herself on the drawing-room soffer, and she said the lady would think she didn't sit there, only in the parlour. I've no patience to write more.

CRYSTAL PALACE.

DEAR LADY COMMISSIONER,—I would like to say a few words about two things, and one is *dressing-time.* Now I believe in all proper houses the servants have that time, but I know in small places the mistress hurries the servants up and down as if she was slave-driving. Every servant ought to have one or two hours to herself every day, besides the time she sits over her meals. Two hours to herself is all right, and that she ought to get to dress herself. Of course I mean she should mend her clothes and do all she has to do for herself in that time. I have lived under a house-keeper and under a mistress, and I liked the housekeeper best, for she did not worry me like my mistress. Then I would like to say a word about the holes some servants sleep in, even in grand houses. I would like you to see some of them, but the mistresses might object. I didn't see any mention of this in "Mistresses *versus* Servants." I give my name, to be kept secret.

ONE THAT HAS RAISED HERSELF.

I slept in the kitchen in my two first places, and three in one bed in another situation, and when we stood on the bed we could touch the ceiling.

PARLOUR-MAID.

MADAM,—The Bible says we are not to serve with "eye-service, as men-pleasers," but I must say I would rather serve two masters than one mistress. My master and mistress have agreed to live separate, and since mistress went away we servants have had a proper life. She used to treat us like dirt, but master lets two of us go out a walk every afternoon, and we have a nice room upstairs to sit in. Ladies seem to think it's only themselves who want fresh air, and they let us poor servants live in dark holes not fit for dogs, let alone women. I've heard our coachman say his horses are better taken care of than us servants. That was before mistress went away. Now we have the same dinner as master, and we choose our own puddings. He ordered pigeon-pie one Sunday when he was going out for dinner, because he thought it would make a change for us servants. I say, "Long may he live, and may there be many like him."

KENSINGTON.

CHAPTER XIV

EMIGRATION FOR SERVANTS.

"IT'S useless for you to say nothing to me, 'Arry; I've signed it with my blood, and Lucy Thomas, she's done the same, and we're going to send it to a lawyer to be witnessed, so it's all done in a business-like and proper fashion. If you're not married when I come back, I'll think about it, but I's going to see the world, I is, I's not always going to stay here. I's not going to marry and have a lot of children. I's going to have my fling first. There, 'Arry, don't be silly."

This extraordinary statement was overheard by a Commissioner a few weeks ago on the top of a City omnibus.

The speaker, a smartly dressed young woman, was sitting beside a young man of the ordinary billy-cock, short coat, light trouser fashion. He, 'Arry, had his arm round her waist, and when she begged him not to "be silly" he removed it, pulled the billy-cock over his eyes, and gave a growl of dissatisfaction.

The young woman had made up her mind to emigrate, and she continued to expatiate on the glories of Queensland, the money she could earn there, and the many sweethearts she was sure to find waiting for her. 'Arry lighted his pipe, and sulked until she began to coax him in feminine fashion, whereupon he declared that there were many pretty girls in London, and if she went away he could find some one else, she need not trouble herself, her offer to marry him when she came back was "quite uncalled for."

London servants, and in fact young women all over the United Kingdom, seem quite to have lost their fear of the water and of foreign countries.

Mr. Clement Scott expressed his surprise at this when he visited the *Jumna*, and saw the young emigrants arriving there "as cheerful and happy as young people can well be."

He says: "I turned to my companion with surprise, asking, 'Where are the tears and sighs, the weeping and the wailing, the sorrow for leaving the old country, that I confidently expected? Where are the forlorn creatures with their scraps of garden-soil conveyed in pocket-handkerchiefs in order to plant a bit of home over there? Where are the sentimental girls with an old rose-bush done up in a parcel and bedewed with tears? I can find no trace of anguish here.'

"'No, they are not crying now, my friend,' was the reply; 'they have got over it. All their tears and lamentations have been left at Blackwall in the Emigrants' Home.'"

Every month a ship leaves England with about two hundred women on board for Queensland, and sometimes fourteen ships carry women over there in the year. The Government of Queensland spends over a million a year on emigration; and the cry is still, "Send us more servants." Any young woman with good health and good character can get a free passage if she is not over thirty-five years of age; if above that age she is called upon to pay £5 towards her passage, but £1 of this goes towards her kit. Each girl must buy her kit at a cost of £1, for it has been found that infection is thus avoided, also all danger of vermin. But the kit is worth £1 17*s.* at the least, and the girl has the benefit of it afterwards, so there is nothing to grumble at. Mrs. Caroline Blanchard, the Hon. Sec. of the Colonial Emigration Society, has kindly furnished us with full information about emigration for servants. This lady has lived in the colonies herself, and is an agent of the Queensland Government. She tells us that English mistresses object very strongly to her Society, for they say that good servants are scarce in England, and that it is a mistake to send away young English women. But Mrs. Blanchard finds that those servants who can command good wages in England do not care to leave the mother country, only girls of the class of *general servants.* Considering that over-population is the *crux* of the female labour question, Mrs. Blanchard is convinced that her society is at the present time doing good service, and we are inclined to agree with her. It may be a mistake to encourage able-bodied men to emigrate, but England (especially London) is well-nigh choked with young women.

Mrs. Blanchard tells us that the girls are eager to go. Formerly they were deterred from emigrating by dread of the voyage, and fear of not getting a situation when they landed. But now many have friends out there, and others have read long accounts of colonial life, so they do not hesitate to leave England. Moreover, they feel the sharp competition that goes on here, and they recognise the fact that it is wiser to go away than to stay where they are not wanted.

The following true anecdotes show the openings that there are for young women who emigrate.

A Queensland Government matron who had been out to the colony many times, with batches of from sixty to one hundred and twenty young women under her charge, writes :—"We stop at the following ports—Malta, Port Said, Aden, Colombo, Batavia. After leaving Batavia, our next stopping place is a pretty but lonely little island called 'Thursday Island,' which forms one of a group of seven islands, named by Captain Cook after the days of the week. It is also the principal pearl-fishing station of the Straits. Two or three voyages ago the resident Government agent came to me to find two general servants. I had no one booked for the island, but asked some of them if they would volunteer to land there ; he not only offered them the high wages of twenty shillings a week, but, among other inducements, told them that there were seven eligible young bachelors on the island, each having £10 a month, and only two unmarried women, whom the said bachelors were cutting each other's throats about ; that he would like to take two young women back with him, if only to restore peace."

On this island is a woman who went out young as a free emigrant in the *Storm King* as a domestic servant. She is now owner of the best hotel there, and possesses five pearl-fishing boats, sending her commodities to the London market. She says she can clear out any day with £15,000; but as she is a widow with five children, she thinks it wiser to stay and protect the business for them.

Her simple story runs thus: "I worked hard for two years in service in the bush, then married a working man. We rode two hundred miles across country to some diggings, set up a store, made money, came to Thursday Island, built an hotel, and went in for the pearl fishery, and met with the success recorded above, living comfortably and bringing up our family respectably."

Full information about emigration can be obtained from Mrs. Blanchard, Colonial Emigration Society, 9, Adelphi Terrace, W.C. She says that servants are in demand in *all* of the colonies, but especially in Queensland. She can promise a free passage to Queensland, and good wages on arrival there, to all respectable young women willing to emigrate. A doctor and a matron accompany the ships, and the girls are looked after until they obtain situations. At Brisbane the depôt is besieged by mistresses directly the ship arrives, and in a few hours not a girl can be had for love or money.

The *Dacca* left England in the summer of 1888 with over two hundred girls on board, bound for Brisbane. Our Commissioners visited the Emigrants' Home the night before she started, and went down to Tilbury with Captain Almond, whose business it is to send away emigrants. The Queensland Government seems to be exceptionally fortunate in its selection of agents and supervising officers. It is impossible to speak too highly of Mrs. Blanchard, whose kindness to the girls makes them feel, although they have only seen her a few times before they sail, that they are leaving behind them a friend—almost a relation. Captain Almond has carried his labours on behalf of emigrants almost to a science, both in the Home at Blackwall and also on board the Government steamers. At the same time one feels that all is being done for the emigrants in relation to their new life in the new country, that the old country is being pushed altogether into the background. Our Commissioners say that it gave them quite a shock to watch over two hundred fine young Englishwomen hurrying away from the mother country without a sigh or a tear, glad to go, and determined that nothing shall bring them back again. When the tender reached the *Dacca* these girls looked like a garden of poppies, for at the Home is a small store, and there the maidens had bought straw hats trimmed with muslin, and ornamented with red flowers, for the modest sum of *9d.* each. A prettier, healthier, happier set of girls it is quite impossible to see anywhere. "Unmarried women first," sang out Captain Almond.

Then Mr. Wilkie, the manager of the Emigrants' Home at Blackwall, sent the girls one by one from the tender to the big ship, where they were received by the doctor and the matron. The foreign crew helped the girls to carry their goods and chattels into the unmarried women's quarters, which are shut off from the rest of the ship, and the girls streamed into their cabins. Each girl was supplied with a small sack containing enough clothes to last her for a fortnight, and many of them carried folding chairs, which can be had at the Home very cheap. A strong smell of roast beef pervaded the cabins, and no sooner were the girls off the tender than the cooks began to serve up a dinner provided by the Queensland Government.

We have not space to give a full description here of the accommodation provided for these young women; but our Commissioners speak of the order and cleanliness of the lower deck. Each girl finds her kit on the cabin bed, and when this is undone she discovers herself possessed of a good flock pillow and mattress, a thick blanket, a box of soap, tins for her meals, and everything that is necessary for her comfort during her six weeks' voyage. The girls are divided into messes, and each mess has a captain ; over all are the matron and the doctor. Books and games are provided, and everything is done to make the girls feel at home ; they are even allowed to choose their cabin companions.

One upper deck is devoted to them, and the only rule they have to keep is this—they must not stray away from their quarters without permission. But they may receive visits from their friends among the single men and the married people, whose quarters are on the other side of the saloon, and nothing is left undone that can increase their comfort. Their bugbear is sea-sickness, but even this does not seem to affect their spirits. All these girls go out to Queensland as servants, but if they are willing to work, and can prove that they have been in domestic service, no inquiries are made about their social position. So they vary in station from Bridget, whose father digs "taties," to the handsome girl from Norfolk, who says that her intention is to make her way in the new country. These girls are the pick of our young countrywomen, and Captain Almond looks at them with satisfaction, saying, "The Government pays us to provide them with good material."

But it is a serious fact that while English girls hurry out of London, foreign girls of an inferior physique come in to take their places. We get the refuse of the Continent in their stead, and as "the youth of a nation are the trustees of posterity," it is a bad look-out for the next generation.

The Emigrants' Home at Blackwall is the work of Captain Almond and others. We all know how emigrants were fleeced in former days, how they sold the very clothes from off their backs to buy food and lodging. The girls are received in this home free of expense, provided with beds, food, and good advice gratis. Lord Radstock and his friends go down the night before they sail to hold a prayer-meeting, and many people say that the emigrants' hymns cannot be heard twice, because they affect the lachrymal glands in an unpleasant manner. It is a wonderful sight to see those five or six hundred men and women singing! The girls are light-hearted enough, but the older people have to break away from many ties, and the memory of these things makes their voices tremulous. They gather together in the great hall of the Home that last night in old England, having said good-bye to their homes, their friends and relations, and their sad faces show little confidence or hope. But the girls look quite different. They think of the high wages in Brisbane, the £40 and £50 a year they can earn up-country. Many of them have friends or relations in Queensland, and not a few are eager for a life of adventure.

It may be said that emigration does not come within our province. But all classes of working women here suffer from the fact that the supply of female labour greatly exceeds the demand at present, so we cannot confer upon the girls in whom we are interested a greater boon than that of showing them a way of escape out of this metropolis.

CHAPTER XV.

FACTORY-GIRLS.

FACTORY-GIRLS are divided by all who have intimate knowledge of them, and by the girls themselves, into two classes—factory-girls proper and girls who work at trades—*i.e.*, City work-girls. This may be considered an arbitrary distinction, but it exists nevertheless, and the girl who works at a trade would be very much offended if any one called her a factory hand, although she comes under the Factory Act.

A curious instance of this distinction has attracted our notice. The eight homes for working girls which have been established throughout London by Mr. John Shrimpton are open to all "homeless" girls, and the low charges made in them for board and lodging are as follows—2*s.*, 2*s.* 6*d.*, and 4*s.* per week for bedroom, including use of dining-room and sitting-rooms, with library; 4*s.* 6*d.* per week for breakfast, dinner, and tea; or separate meals at 2½*d.* for breakfast, *6d.* for dinner, $2\frac{1}{2}$*d.* for tea, and $1\frac{1}{2}$*d.* for supper.

These homes are the greatest blessings the working girls of the metropolis possess, and are frequented by girls engaged in all sorts of trades, as well as by shop-girls and milliners. But the factory-girl proper does not enter them, or if she does so by mistake, three days find her outside their doors again. Her purse does not permit her to stay, and her nature is such that she cannot bear any restraint, any approach to order and discipline.

The factory-girl proper ranks next to the flower-girl or the street-seller in the social scale, and constantly she falls into the ranks of the hawker-race. She picks hops and fruit in the summer, and does odd jobs when work is slack. Instead of the casual, she has the unskilled labourer for a father, while the City work-girl is generally the daughter of an artisan.

Readers would probably be very much astonished if they knew how difficult it is to get accurate information about the girls who come under the Factory Act. These girls make everything, from the beautifully-bound book in the library of the student to the match in Bryant and May's factory, about which we have heard so much lately. We shall deal first with the factory-girl proper the child of the unskilled labourer, and then pass on to the City work-girl, the daughter of the artisan.

We may safely say that the average wage of the factory-girl proper is from 4*s.* to 8*s.* a week throughout London. Some earn more than 8*s.*, a few earn less than 4*s.*; but if we take them *en masse* their wage is from 4*s.* to 8*s.* per week. When they become young women their wages increase, and as forewomen they earn more money; but the factory-girl, who is a drug in the market, gets the pittance of from 4*s.* to 8*s.* a week.

The chief characteristic of the factory-girl is her want of reverence. She has a rough appearance, a hard manner, a saucy tongue, and an impudent laugh. We heard a lady regretting the other day that the factory-girls in her district did not know the difference between the daughter of a peer and the child of a dock-labourer. She had invited the daughter of a well-known evangelical nobleman to see her club, which is attended by at least a hundred and eighty factory-girls, and Lady —— brought a lover with her. The factory girls were tickled by the situation, and in a few minutes the daughter of the evangelical nobleman and the lover had to beat a hasty retreat. This thing is certain: if asked to distinguish between the daughter of a peer and the daughter of a dock-labourer, the factory-girls would call the former "a young person" and the latter "a young lady."

But to see the real disposition of the factory-girl one must watch her with her fellow-workers not with those who consider themselves to be her betters. When she leaves the Board School and shakes off home discipline she is like an untrained colt—she resents all attempts to put her into harness. Those who know anything about girls are aware that at the age of fourteen or fifteen they pass through a stage of sheer "cursedness," at which time they are a terror to mothers and a scourge to governesses if they belong to the upper classes. Now, these factory-girls are like the rest of their sex, only they have no governesses to dog their heels, no mammas to talk to them about the laws that govern society, no wish to be fashionable or correct. They either pay their parents for board and lodging or go off to live, three and four together, in a room near their work. It is no uncommon thing to find two girls using a room by day and two more using the same room by night. Such girls are in every sense of the word their own mistresses, and they fiercely resent interference on the part of parents, pastors, masters, or any one else. But the girl who turns her back on parents and family, who cheeks her employers, and laughs at passers-by

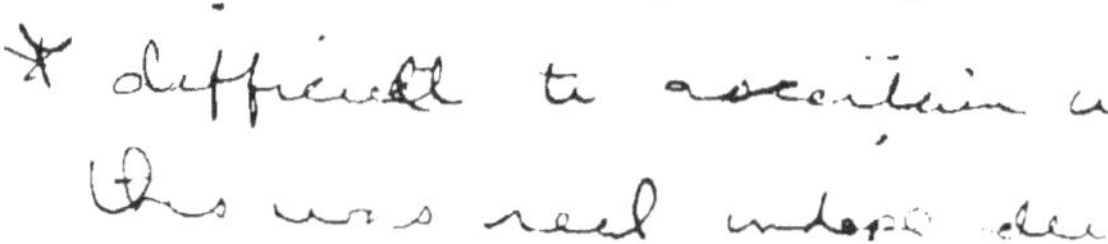

in the street, is like wax when a fellow-worker falls ill or a collection has to be made for a sick companion. She lends her clothes and her boots if a friend can thus get a chance of "bettering herself." She shares her last crust with a girl out of work, and "cries her eyes out" over the grave of a fellow-worker. Among no other class of young women does there appear to be so much camaraderie, such a strong instinct that all must pull together, such a commune of food, clothes, and halfpence as among the factory-girls of the metropolis.

At the time of the strike at Bryant and May's factory a girl was asked why it had taken place.

"Well, it just went like tinder," she said; "one girl began, and the rest said 'yes,' so out we all went."

When the girls were being paid their week's wages in Charrington's Hall on Mile End Waste after the strike, it was curious to see the waves of feeling that rolled over their faces, how all seemed influenced at the same time, and in the same manner, by what was said and done for them. And few people could help being touched by the way in which the girls were determined to stand together at all costs. "I can pawn this for you," "I'll lend you that to take to my uncle's," was heard all about the room; and in every direction girls might be seen plotting how they could help one another on until Bryant and May gave them back their "pennies."

We do not intend to say anything about this strike. Bryant and May's factory is not worse than many other factories in the way it pays its hands. The *worst* paid factory-girls are those who work in places where butter-scotch and other sweet stuffs are made; the *best* paid factory-girls are those who make cigars and cigarettes

A butter-scotch factory, that employs many girls, pays as follows. The girls begin with 2*s.* 6*d.* per week, and 6*d.* good conduct money; the elder girls earn from 5*s.* to 7*s.* 6*d.* per week. This factory was formerly further north, and when it moved into its present neighbourhood, twelve of the best girls struck for an extra 2*d.* per day to pay for their omnibus. They were told that the firm could get girls in the neighbourhood, so they all had to give in and go back. Work begins at 8.15 a.m.; and if a girl is late she is fined 7*d.*; an hour is allowed for dinner, after which the girls go on working until 6 p.m. Saturday brings a half holiday, of course, the girls being paid at 2 p.m., or at 1.30, according to the whim of the brothers who manage the place. The girls complain bitterly of the "drilling" that is practised in this factory. There are many kinds of drill, from keeping a girl standing an hour to half the day or more ; but the drilling she finds hardest to bear is a week's holiday, for then she has to meet the anger of parents, or to bear the pangs of hunger. A day's illness sometimes means drill for a week.

This is a fair specimen of the lowest-class factory, to which flock girls who have just passed the Fourth Standard. Girls like sweetstuff, and they are generally allowed "to get a sickening," after which they do not eat much, but they generally have a sickly appearance. One of the saddest sights in the metropolis is to see such girls being "taken on" on a Monday morning. They struggle for work, and "slang" the manager ; they use the most awful language, and act like little maniacs. The manager could get them to work for almost nothing, only then they would faint at their work, and be useless. The stories these girls tell of their privations must touch the stoniest heart, and make the firmest believer in competition suffer from qualms of conscience. A tobacco factory near Saffron Hill is a good specimen of the highest class of factories. The girls begin there with 3*s.* a week, and are allowed 6*d.* per hundred cigars directly they can use their fingers. They are apprenticed for four years, after which time they receive 9*d.*, 1*s.*, 1*s.* 6*d.*, and 2*s.* per hundred cigars, according to the quality of their work. They can make from one to three hundred cigars in the day, and their wages vary from 8*s.* to 23*s.* per week. The girls who are especially skilful make more than this. The manager says that the work is not suitable for women, because the strong smell of the tobacco affects their health; and the work requires so much practice. "I've had three or four girls in a dead faint all at once," he said. "And I've got to keep a bottle of sal volatile on the place. Then, directly they've got their hand well in, they go and get married. We've men here that have been from fifteen to forty years on the place. Girls are so easily upset." These girls work from 9 a.m. to 6 p.m., with an hour off for dinner. They have no fines, and are under a very popular forewoman. The happiness of factory-girls depends very much on the head forewoman—or, as she is generally called, the labour-mistress. She is generally chosen from among the staff of forewomen, but sometimes she is a school-mistress who has broken down in health, the widow of a tradesman, or some one of that description. The "hands" prefer a woman who has been trained on the place, and who thoroughly understands the business.

Factory-girls vary very much in different parts of the metropolis; and any one who knows the genus well can say at once which quarter of London a factory-girl comes from by her appearance. The East End girl is rough, and indulges in vulgar horse-play with lads of her own age. She frequents penny-gaffs with her "round-the-corner" (sweėtheart), and lets him treat her to beer in the public-house. Occasionally she visits the pit of a theatre, and cracks nuts there with her teeth between the acts. The West End girl is vicious; she speaks a lingo which only her friends can understand, sings songs which have a hidden meaning, and has an unpleasant way of carrying on dual conversations, one sentence aloud to the general public, another in an undertone for the benefit of a companion. Midway between these two is the girl who lives in the slums of the West Central district. They all wear the same uniform; a draggled, dark-coloured skirt, which is covered up with an apron while in the factory; a long black jacket bought by weekly instalments of a shilling or sixpence; and a black hat trimmed with a gorgeous feather. A wisp of hair behind and a heavy fringe in front is the approved head-dress. This one may see in Bermondsey, Southwark, Hackney, and other outlying districts, as well as in the City.

A great deal is done for these girls in different parts of London. Many clubs are held for them, and they are sent into the country, either by private funds or in connection with fresh-air missions. Mrs. De Fontaine's club in Southwark, Miss Canney's club in Hatton Garden, and a dozen others have been visited by our Commissioners. The latest attempt to help the girls is, of course, in connection with Trades Unions, and as these are beginning to prove a success we may hope to see further attempts at combination among factory-girls in different districts of the metropolis. Girls meet with accidents every day in these factories. We have heard of a ginger-beer factory in which they have one accident a week, such as getting an eye blown out, and where the girls never think of claiming damages. It is the same in places where girls make fireworks ; and in many cases the managers take advantage of their employées' ignorance. Messrs. Bryant and May's girls are developing a faculty for business ; so no doubt there are the same powers of organization among other factory-girls of London.

The homes of these girls are, as a rule, very wretched. One or two rooms, which they share with father, mother, brothers, and sisters, a general purse, out of which they sometimes get a shilling on Saturday night, a dirty court—these are the things they mean by "home." So many men are now out of work that these girls become in many cases breadwinners for the whole family. The description of one "home" will be sufficient.

Across Blackfriars Bridge, in a street at the back of the first church, lives a girl of seventeen with her bedridden mother. She earns 10*s.* a week in a feather factory, where she works from 8 a.m. to 6 p.m., with an hour off for dinner. After six o'clock she returns home to do the housework. She is an out-patient at one of the London hospitals. The room costs 5*s.* a week, so the mother and daughter have 2*s.* 6*d.* each a week to live upon. The room is clean, but heaped up with boxes, and on washing day the fumes almost stifle the sick woman. A flower or two in the window, a book from the parish library, are the only comforts these poor things possess, yet one never hears a word of complaint. The girl sometimes says that she finds her work monotonous; but adds, "It's nothing like what mother has to put up with."

It is useless to pretend that factory-girls have much religious feeling or high moral principles. Some have, the greater number have not. On Sunday they liein bed all morning, and go for a walk with their "round-the-corner" after dinner. Their theory seems to be "it's all right if you're not found out;" and their love-making rarely means marriage.

CHAPTER XVI.

CITY WORK-GIRLS.

WE do not mean to say that the factory-girl proper cannot be found among those who term themselves "City work-girls;" in fact, we have come across her again and again working amongst them. But she is not of them. Any one who has studied the young women of the metropolis can pick her out in a minute if she strays into their ranks, for she belongs to another genus. City work-girls ply over two hundred distinct employments, to say nothing of the hundred and one odd trades which could not be carried on without their help, at any rate could not be carried on with so much profit.

We will give a few examples of these employments:—Bookbinder and folder, brush maker, button maker, compositor, electric light fitter, gentleman's cravat maker, gold and silver burnisher, indiarubber stamp machinist, instrument coverer, leather bag maker, muff liner, spectacle maker, surgical instrument maker, umbrella maker, straw worker, gun-cap maker, harness maker, maltine weigher, crystallising glass photo-frame maker, portmanteau worker, perfumer, pattern card mounter, magic lantern slide maker, etc., etc.

Half a century ago the trades open to women were very few. Needles were almost the only implements they could handle in order to gain their living. Now commerce admits women into almost all of its branches; and although they are heavily handicapped, we see female labourers pushing on in every direction. They are forming Trades Unions, and making friends with workers of the other sex, who begin to think that, if the work is the same, the pay should be equal. The day on which the London Trades Council came forward as the friend of the match-girls formed an epoch in the history of the female labour market. Men are beginning to realize that they must work with women and not against them, for the thin edge of the wedge has gone into the masculine conscience. Besides, the men see that they must get the good-will of the women if they want to shut out the children, to cut off the last resource of the capitalist in his greed for profit. Self-interest is at the bottom of most things, and since the example has been set by the London Trades Unionists, men throughout the country are beginning to pose as the champions of the weaker sex. Human motives are very mixed, so, while we recognise the chivalry of men in helping forward the interests of female labour, we must not be blind to the fact that both sexes are beginning to see very plainly that "like as the arrows in the hand of the giant, even so are the young children" in the hands of the capitalist.

Women who wish to form a Trades Union, or who are interested in this subject, and desire to know more about it, are advised to write to Miss Clementina Black, secretary of the Women's Provident League and Trades Union, Industrial Hall, Clark's Buildings, Broad Street, W.C.

The wages of City work-girls vary from 8*s.* to 14*s.* per week. Some earn much more, few earn less; but taking "slack times" into consideration, 8*s.* to 14*s.* are their wages.

"Slack time" is the bugbear of the City work-girl. If the work were regular she would be a fairly happy individual; but she does not earn enough to put by, and, although she knows pretty well when the slack season will set in, she cannot provide for it. Supposing she is a London girl her family help her, and she makes her clothes during slack weeks, or assists her mother in household matters; but, if she is a stranger in the metropolis, she pawns her clothes, and falls back upon other means of subsistence. It is a curious fact that, although most of these girls belong to the artisan class, the greater number of them are not Londoners ; they come from all parts of the United Kingdom to pick up the gold which is still supposed to pave the streets of the metropolis. Very few go back to tell the tale of the great City; so girls daily flock into our Modern Babylon from small towns and country villages. Two girls, friends, have come under our notice. They were discontented with their life in a small market town in the South of England, and came to London to make their fortune. They took a room in the West Central district, and began to look for work. On applying at various places they were told "No hands are wanted ;" and at others they heard, "We never take girls who have not been properly taught, country hands are of no use to us." Bit by bit they pawned all their clothes, and still they walked from place to place looking for work. One day they met their old employer, who had come to London on business. He was shocked to see how thin they had become, to notice their ragged clothes and anxious appearance. He offered to take them back, for they had good characters, and had given him satisfaction during the years they had worked for him. But they were too proud to give in They could not let their friends in the market town see that they had no value in the great City. They refused his offer with tears, he says; but they went on their way, and he never saw them again. Within a year from that time these girls were dead. One died from the effect of drugs given to her by a chemist; the other died in childbirth.

If parents, clergymen, and those in authority throughout the United Kingdom would realize the fact, and impress it upon girls, that in London at the present time there is a plethora of young women, it would be a great blessing. Such people are apt to think, if work is difficult to get in country districts, a girl is sure to find something to do in London. They merely send a girl to damnation if they help her to swell the numbers of the London girls who now compete for a living. These London girls find the struggle almost more than they can manage, although they have homes in the metropolis, and friends to fall back upon during slack times. A girl who is a stranger here is the most destitute and helpless individual one can well imagine. Employers prefer London girls, who have, as they say, "all their wits about them and a proper training." So the country competitors tramp from place to place seeking employment; and if they do get work they lose it again, for they cannot tide over slack times.

They have no friends to fall back upon, no homes to live in during the weeks and months in which no one can give them employment.

There is one trade in London that has no slack time for women, and the number of those who ply it is said to be no less than 100,000. Their number was some years ago 80,000, but now 20,000 more have joined it. City work-girls do not add to its number openly, but they swell the numbers of those women who carry on a hidden trade to eke out their wages. This hidden trade has recruits among all classes of young women in London, from the pretty, neatly dressed little governess who trips into the precincts of the Law Courts on Saturday night, to the flower-girl who would swear until black in the face if she heard herself accused of anything so nefarious.

We have decided not to speak of the open traffic; but the hidden trade must be mentioned in connection with these City work-girls.

No one supposes that young men in Tempted London live the lives of celibates until those days when fortune gives them money enough to be married. Moreover, it is a fact that large numbers of these young men are *encouraged by their parents* to form relationships with young women—relationships of a more or less permanent character, but which are not intended to end in marriage. The girls, no doubt, expect to attach the men to themselves permanently; but to the honour of the men it must be said that they give no reason for such hopes, and let the girls clearly understand what is meant by such relationships. We need not say here *why* mothers and fathers encourage these proceedings; but that they do so we have full evidence. The girls fall into no trap, for the men help to eke out their wages, and add to the brightness of their lives by tickets for theatres, visits to music-halls, novelettes, and gifts of jewellery and dresses. These poor girls *must* make a smart appearance. If they receive more wages than the factory-girl proper, it is because their employers insist on a smart appearance. The factory-girl's dress costs next to nothing, but the City work-girl must starve herself, and go without proper under-clothing, in order to buy the smart clothes which make the ignorant think her well-off and extravagant. An example is better than further description.

We sent a Commissioner into a lodging-house about ten minutes' walk from the City, which is frequented by clerks earning about £2 a week, and by girls engaged in various employments, *i.e.*, City work-girls. This house holds over forty people. Rooms in it vary from 7*s.* 6*d.* a week to 3*s.* 6*d.* The City work-girl pays usually 3*s.* 6*d.* for a room by herself; but her habit is to engage a room at 5*s.* per week, and share it with a companion. The same fire and lights then do for both, also the same fee to the slavey who waits upon such establishments. There are various other economies connected with these 5*s.* arrangements which we forget; but the room is generally large, furnished with a bed, horse-hair sofa, and armchair, three or four chairs, a table, and a chest of drawers. On the wall are some prints, and on the fireplace a few china ornaments. Each lodger has a latch-key. Meals are served in the bedroom. Our Commissioner engaged a room at 5*s.* a week, next to two City work-girls, who had then been two years in the house. She was introduced to these "young ladies" by the landlady the first night, when one of them was carrying up supper—two red herrings, some beer, bread, and red cabbage pickle. Both of these girls had sweethearts, young men who came in the evening and stayed until one or two o'clock in the morning. Sometimes one girl went to the theatre or a music-hall with her sweetheart, and the other remained at home with her sweetheart to make a dress or trim a hat. Then beer was fetched, or a bottle of wine, and those at home had what the girls called a quiet evening. On Sunday the sweethearts arrived before the girls were up, and stayed all day, paying for their own dinner. After the sweethearts went away, at one or two o'clock in the morning, the lodgers upstairs or downstairs paid the girls visits, stopping in their room until six or seven o'clock. While our Commissioner was there, one girl quarrelled with her sweetheart, and took a lodger in his place. It is needless to say that the girls received money and presents from these young men, besides being treated by them to places of entertainment and to outings. The girls were not Londoners—one had come from Norfolk, the other from the North of England. They had made friends in London, and worked near one another, but not at the same employment. They talked of their sweethearts in a frank, easy way, and also of other things connected with their mode of life, which we cannot make public. These girls would have been horrified if any one had suggested that the State and the Church would class them with prostitutes.

Our Commissioner asked the landlady if she considered it right to let young men come and go at all hours of the day and night. The answer was—

"Lor', they're the girls' sweethearts."

And when it was suggested to this worthy individual that her lodgers led a careless sort of life in her house, she said,

"Well, but the young men wouldn't stay if I interfered with 'em. Young people will be young people. It isn't my business."

This house is especially recommended by the clergy of the district.

We do not mean to say that City work-girls ply the hidden trade more than other girls; but the fact that so many of them are strangers in London, living in rooms, and unprotected, makes them more inclined to become the mistresses of young men who cannot afford to marry, and who do not care to associate with common prostitutes. These girls *must* live. Their wages are low, owing to the fact that there are in London too many of them, and slack times force them to do things they would prefer to leave undone.

CHAPTER XVII.

CITY WORK-GIRLS.

(*Continued.*)

THE girls often fall into the relationships we have described in order to eke out their low wages ; but oftener still these things are the result of slack times. There is *this* difference between the work of women and men. While the latter say, "I cannot dig ; to beg I am ashamed," the former have a trade to fall back upon that has no slack times, that is always sure to bring in a living. "C'est le premier pas qui coûte."

The girls soon become callous. One of them told a Commissioner the other day that she was saving up the money she received from her sweethearts in order to marry.

"You see," she said, "I can easily get a husband if I save up enough."

Many of these self-dependent girls are homeless orphans, or have been turned adrift by step-parents. Others are girls who cannot get work in the country, and who think they can make their own way in London. At any rate, City work-girls who have no friends in the metropolis ought to be pitied more than blamed, if they live as we have stated.

Ruskin says, "The most directly necessary charity in England is to save poor girls from distress, overwork, and surrounding evils."

Homeless, friendless, motherless, a class of which society is only just beginning to realise the existence, these girls cannot be expected to pass their lives in want and loneliness while young men are willing to spend money on them.

A poor girl who had been out of work for nearly six months, and living by herself in a wretched garret, told a Commissioner the other day :—

"Gentlemen are the only people who speak to me civil."

A great many people interest themselves in these girls, and many societies work amongst them ; but such things do not alter the facts that lie at the root of their difficulties. Low wages, slack times, the rush and drive of competition, the over-population, which produces a "lost-in-the-mass" sort of feeling, cannot be altered by a few benevolent people and religious societies. These facts require the careful consideration and prompt action of those who boast of progress and science.

> "It is well that while we range with Science, glorying in the time,
> City children soak and blacken soul and sense in City slime!
> There, among the gloomy alleys, Progress halts on palsied feet,
> Crime and hunger cast our maidens by the thousand on the street!
> There the master scrimps his haggard sempstress of her daily bread,
> There a single sordid attic holds the living and the dead!"

The girl-labour question is but a portion of the larger labour question which will, when the Irish question is settled, attract practical politicians; until then, it is the business of all to get accurate information on the subject, and to point out in which direction things connected with labour are moving at present. Girls are the cheapest sort of labour-force employers can get; they would, if they could, work for nothing. No wonder, then, that the capitalist takes advantage of them, and that their weekly wage is a few shillings. We have not space to notice their different employments; but we must draw attention to the way in which they are over-worked and undor paid in some printing establishments.

Girls look for vacant places in printers' and

publishers' establishments in the daily papers, also outside certain shops, where the following advertisements may be seen every Monday, and round them an eager, excited group of young women :—

"Folders and sewers wanted." "Folders wanted at once." "Vellum sewer wanted." "Good vellum sewers at once."

The pay is generally per thousand sheets. At a large establishment near Fleet Street the girls work from 8 a.m. to 8 p.m., with an hour for dinner, and half an hour for tea if they like to forfeit their tea-time in wages. The gas is on full in this place, for the rooms are old and dark. Into some of the rooms it is impossible to walk upright ; and there is little ventilation, no sanitary arrangements, no attempt to provide the girls with a room during their dinner hour. The girls receive at the end of the first six months a bonus of 14*s.* During the second six months they are paid at half-price. After the first year they receive 4*d.* per thousand sheets.

At an establishment where one of the largest London papers is printed, girls are paid 5*d.* and 6*d.* per hour, and an extra penny after 10 p.m. At this place they often begin at 6 a.m., and work until 12 p.m. Sometimes they are kept on all night, sewing and folding, going home at 6 a.m. for breakfast. Of course this is not lawful, but the factory inspectors are few, and easily hoaxed. They seldom insist on seeing the wage-book, which is the only way of getting at the truth. When the girls work all night at this place, they get an extra 5*s*., which pleases them so much they would swear black is white if the inspector came across them. They think it is a joke to hide when a message is sent up that the inspector is coming, and run out in order "to do him," as they call it. Far from perceiving that he protects their interests, they look on him as an intruder and an enemy. The book-sewers employed by religious publishers are proverbially underpaid. Mr. Lakeman, H.M. Inspector for the Central Metropolitan District, says, in his report of 1887, at page 90: 'Religious publications are very poorly paid for; piecework rules, and masters accept orders on the barest margin of profits. . . . I believe that publishers' binding work is now among the poorest paid of City industries."

He adds:—"It is undisputed that great and sore trials are undergone by many young hands out of season. I am told that the struggle comes with heavy temptations: some who cannot be helped at home, or who have no homes, are obliged to seek cheap lodgings, where companions are met who, being stronger and more skilful, lead them on step by step till the *facile descensus* is complete."

Mr. Lakeman's statement bears out our own conclusions ; and although many occupations pay city girls much better than folding and sewing, slack times and low wages, with over-work, lead many of them into sorry circumstances. The workers he speaks about earn, while learners, from 3*s.* to 4*s.* a week ; and when experienced hands, from 12*s.* to 15*s.* Their work is uncertain. The ordinary slack season is from March to July, and there are also "extra" slack seasons, when many are dispensed with.

A lady wrote a letter on the subject of religious publications to a paper after Mr. Lakeman's statements appeared, in which she said :—

"It would be terrible indeed if our cheap Bibles, cheap tracts, and cheap moral stories are cheap through the sacrifice of girls' souls and bodies."

We quite agree with her that Mr. Lakeman's charge is "very serious ;" but even Mr. Lakeman is only half awake at present.

CHAPTER XVIII.

EAST END SHIRT-MAKERS.

WE are speaking here of shirts made of harvard and flannelette, which are used by working men throughout the metropolis. Harvard is very unpleasant material to sew, because it is so stiff; but flannelette, which has been four or five years in fashion, is soft and pleasant. The workers are divided into two classes: first, the *machinists*, the women who make the shirt; secondly, the *finishers*, who fasten off the cottons, make the button-holes, sew on the buttons, etc. The latter are unskilled workers, and their work is the lowest class of labour in connection with the shirt business. These finishers are paid by sweaters 3*d.* or 3½*d.* per dozen for common shirts, or about *one farthing each.* They find their own thread. In many cases they walk long distances to get the work and take it back, and often they are kept waiting by their employers.

They are also subject to fines for delay in

taking the work home, and for other offences against the sweaters' code; and they never get work on a Monday, seldom get work on a Friday or Saturday. Tuesday, Wednesday, and Thursday are the sweaters' days of business. There are in East London no less than 2,000 sweaters, and the people they sweat worst of all are the unfortunate finishers of common shirts.

The machinists receive from *6d.* to *8d.* per dozen for common shirts, finding their own cotton, which costs them about 1*d.* per two dozen shirts. They also are subject to fines, and must take long journeys to fetch their work and carry it back.

The scale of payment for working-men's shirts of a better quality is much the same—that is to say, the sweaters take the same proportion of profits. A shirt that is made for less than 1*d.* is sold at 1*s.* 1*d.* to the working man. His wife could not possibly make it so cheap, unless she happened to have a sewing machine. A clever finisher can do three dozen shirts per day, but the ordinary worker can only do two dozen, thus earning about *6d.* per day, or 3*s.* a week.

A clever machinist might do two dozen shirts of the lowest make, but in most cases she does one dozen, or one dozen and a half, thus earning about 1*s.* 4*d.* per day, or 9*s.* 4*d.* per week.

The trade is often very slack, and few

workers get as many shirts to make as they would like, consequently some of the worst cases of poverty in the East End are found among the shirt-makers.

Nearly all the work is done at home, but occasionally the women work in a sweater's den, where eight or ten women sit in a small room without any ventilation. The improvers, or girls who are learning the shirt business, may sometimes be found in these wretched places, but generally they work at home, beginning at 8 a.m. and leaving off at 9 p.m.

The home of a finisher is thus described by a Commissioner :—

"I went to see a shirt finisher in Stepney, and found her rejoicing over a dozen shirts that had come in after long waiting, and, as she said, 'a deal of prayer.' She lives in a room on the ground floor, at the back of the house—a small, dark place, without much furniture. Her bed is made of boxes, an old mattress, and a piece of sacking. She had no fire when I called, and she had no food ; but she did not complain while she sat at her work, although she shivered so much that she could scarcely hold her needle. She was anxious to get the work done to carry it home, in order to buy some food. An old table stood near the window, and she explained that she worked in a draught because she could not afford a light. The shirts would bring her in 4½*d.* when finished; but she could not take them to the sweater before the next morning, so she must go to bed without any supper, or rather lie awake under the bit of sacking, thinking how much she could buy with 4½*d.*"

We are indebted to Mr. W. J. Walker for the above information about prices paid to the machinists and finishers. Mr. Walker has devoted much time to investigating East End shirt-making, and is deeply interested in the unfortunate needle-women. He is one of the directors of the Workwomen's Co-operative Association, Limited, Walden Street, Commercial Road, E., which is doing much good work in that neighbourhood. The workers call him a "beautiful gentleman," for he has visited them in their homes, and he is one of those who cannot help relieving desperate cases while he is making his scientific investigations. The Association pays 5*d.* and 6*d.* per dozen to finishers, and 1*s.* or 1*s.* 1*d.* to machinists. It has had a very salutary effect on the sweaters of the neighbourhood, by forcing them to raise their rate of payment. We have not space to say more about it here; but it works on sound principles. It goes in for "pure and simple business, based on righteous co-operation."

In the Central Metropolitan District we find shirt-makers paid as follows:—

Shirts, best (machine)—
  Young hands, 6*s*. for six months.
  Experienced workers, 10*s*. to 14*s*. per week.
  Extra clever workers, 18*s*. to 20*s*. per week.
Button-holes (machine)—
  Young hands, 6*s*. for six months.
  Experienced workers, 10*s*. per week.
  Extra clever workers, 15*s*. to 17*s*. per week.
Medium—
  Young hands, 6*s*. for six months.
  Experienced workers, 10*s*. per week.
  Extra clever workers, 12*s*. to 15*s*. per week.
Low class, domestic—
  Women, generally assisted by family, 7*s*. a week.
  Finishing by hand in factory, women, 8*s*. to 12*s*.
  At home finishing, 7*d*. per dozen medium quality; 3*d*. per dozen low quality; 3*s*. 6*d*. to 5*s*. per week.

WEST END SHIRT-MAKERS.

The West End shirt and collar trade is well paid, and the workers say "there is nothing to complain of" in it. The workers seldom take less than 10*s.* a week; and most of them make 17*s.*, 18*s.*, and £1 during the season. It is nearly all piecework, but some of the workers are paid by the day where few are kept. The shirt factories are generally separate from the false collar (those collars not fastened to the shirt) factories, but sometimes both are made in the same factory. The hours are from 9 a.m. to 7 p.m., with an hour for dinner; and half an hour for tea. Also a half-holiday on Saturday. Very little of the West End work is done at home, only the button-holes. Buttoning, *i.e.*, sewing on buttons, is the work of beginners. The slack season lasts from September to the end of November; the season begins in April.

CHAPTER XIX.

BARMAIDS.

THE girls who serve behind the bars of restaurants and buffets, also behind the bars of theatres, hotels, and railway stations, consider themselves a step above ordinary barmaids; namely, the girls who serve in public-houses.

They are all young ladies of course, but the former are designated "the young ladies at the bar," while the latter are "young ladies in the public line of business."

A very telling little pamphlet, under the title of "Called to the Bar," was published some time ago by Miss Beale. This deals with first-class barmaids, and especially with those engaged in the Metropolitan Railway bars, or the "subterranean hotels," as Miss Beale calls them. Of all barmaids these girls are most to be pitied. Draughts, bad atmosphere, and sulphurous smoke give them sore throats and heart complaints. Not a few of them stand from seventy-six to eighty-six hours in the week, or about eleven hours a day. They work in shifts, coming on early in the morning, and working with stated intervals until midnight. One Sunday in the month is considered ample time for recreation. Yet the girls prefer this life to domestic service. They think it more "genteel" to be a barmaid than a servant.

They are seldom allowed to sit down, and they say if they might only have sliding seats to draw back from the bar—rather high, so that they could rest without appearing to sit—they would be less often on the doctor's books. But their employers, with a few exceptions, will not hear of this.

Some of the Metropolitan Railway bars are upstairs; for instance, the one at High Street, Kensington; but not a few are on the underground platform—small, dark places, without ventilation, full of smoke, reeking with alcohol. Let readers think what it means to stand ten, eleven hours in such places day after day, with no rest except on Sunday; to sleep in rooms below the streets, which must be lighted all the twenty-four hours with gas, and which never get a ray of daylight. But the girls say they would rather sleep four or six in such rooms, and two in a bed, than take the last train to another station, for sometimes they miss the train, and then they must walk home—or run, for they are afraid to go slowly through the empty streets at midnight.

Things are not managed much better at some of the largest London stations. At one terminus twenty-two barmaids are employed, with salaries of 8*s.* a week. The manageress receives 17*s.* 6*d.*, and the sub-manageress 10*s.* a week. Each girl is allowed to consume 10*d.* a day in spirits, or 5*s.* 10*d.* a week. This money must be spent in drink, not food; but if the girl is a teetotaler she is allowed ginger-beer or lemonade. The manageress, or her assistant, serves the 10*d.* allowances, and the girls are not supposed to help themselves. Nevertheless, they do it.

It is impossible for any manageress, be she (as the girls say) "ever so much of a cat," to watch all that goes on at the bar of a large station. So the girls cheat the customers if they dare not cheat their employers; and many an innocent customer swallows "waste" while the barmaid drinks his order for spirits. "Waste" is whatever is left in the glasses. This is, by order of the employers, put into the glass measures behind the bar. Each measure has a colour: white for brandy, blue for gin, green for whisky, and red for rum. The "waste" is kept in the measures and served to the customers, for, as the girls say, "We wouldn't touch that muck." So the customers swallow "waste," and the girls drink their orders for spirits.

Barmaids have other ways of getting more than their legitimate ten-pennyworth; but they dare not water the spirits, for if they did, it would certainly be found out. One excuse for this conduct is that their food is very bad. The meat they receive is generally tough, and the butter rancid, to say nothing of stale vegetables and bread. Their work is exhausting, and their little close sitting-rooms behind the bar or beneath the station are not likely to increase their appetites.

Most of them spend half of their money on stout, which is sustaining, and not a few take stout for lunch and for dinner. Some prefer a glass of ale for lunch, a glass of wine in the afternoon, and a glass of spirits when they have done work. The manageress takes gin and bitters, and other "nips," to help her on through the long hours of business.

Board and lodging are provided by the employers. At the terminus we are now speaking about the girls live quite a mile away from their work, and as they must wash up before they go home, it is often midnight before they reach their beds. Some of them complain bitterly of the long walk in winter when the ground is covered with snow, and others say they would not mind so much if the "hangers-on" did not follow them.

These "hangers-on" are the men who use bars as their clubs, who remain in them two or three hours, drinking. Some of them are "horsey" individuals; not a few are flash mobsmen, who go there to discuss business. These girls could, if they would, tell many secrets; but the bar has its code of honour, and they seldom peach. There is only one sin men never condone in women, and that is peaching.

Board and lodging, 5*s.* 10*d.* a week for spirits, and 8*s.* for extras, may seem ample to those readers who forget how well barmaids are supposed to dress, and their heavy bills for washing and breakages. The average weekly bill for a first-class barmaid's breakages is from 1*s.* 6*d.* to 2*s.* She not only has to pay for her own breakages, but for those of customers. In some places there is a regular breakage fund, and a certain amount is deducted from each girl's wages to put into it. This is very hard on the girls, for late at night, when customers get intoxicated, many things are broken. They dare not complain of their customers.

Not long ago three or four young men watched the manageress out of a railway bar, and then went in to have "a lark." They upset the bottles of water, put the napkins in the claret cup, and did other mischief. One of the barmaids ventured to remonstrate. They then complained to her employer that they had not been treated with sufficient courtesy; and the following day all of the girls were discharged at a moment's notice. Barmaids are obliged to put up with a great deal, for if they call in a policeman they are generally bound to charge some one, and this brings disgrace on the business. So they wink at many things, and try to keep their customers in good humour, merely making a few slight objections when a man jumps across the bar to give them a kiss, or wishes to act as an amateur hairdresser. Among barmaids there are of course many fast girls, as there are everywhere else; but all who know them well are aware that a large number of them are quiet, modest women, who work hard, who neither flirt nor drink.

But they must make themselves agreeable, or they are dismissed, and sometimes at a moment's notice. Many managers will only have girls who flirt. Again and again we have heard of girls turned away because they are too steady; and of others who are dismissed because managers think it well to exhibit new faces. "Men get tired of always seeing the same women at the bar," and managers wish to please their customers.

Fifteen to sixteen years of service count in some places for nothing if custom begins to fall off. First, the sub-manageress is removed, then a hint is given to the young ladies. The girls try to look smart; they laugh and chaff, then become reckless. No character is given when they are turned away; and they say to themselves:

"Who will give employment to a discharged barmaid?"

It is not the same everywhere, but in the greater number of places fast girls are preferred, and no questions are asked about what they do when away from the bar—where they get their smart clothes and jewellery. Drinking is the fatal sin of barmaids. They are surrounded by temptations; their hours are long, and their food is bad. It is difficult for them to resist spirits.

"We are most of us half-seas over when we go to bed," said a barmaid who lives in a well-known restaurant. She and her companions have rooms at the top of the house, under the superintendence of an ex-barmaid. The managers sleep on the same landing. In most cases the girls return at night from restaurants, buffets, and theatres to depôts; but in some cases they live on the premises. The age of admittance used to be eighteen, but now it is lower. The distinction made with regard to morality is that "kept" girls are shunned by their more respectable companions. The latter marry men of their own station, or start in the public line of business, while "kept" girls become common prostitutes.

The "kept" girls take tips; but the others rarely accept presents, unless they are Christmas-boxes given to all, not to one in particular. We cannot mention names here, but there are several employers we should like to recommend on account of the care they take about accommodation and food for their young ladies. Their name is not legion, and as yet they do not seem to realise that girls cannot work ten and twelve hours a day without breaking down. At several of the large London stations barmaids are allowed to sit when at leisure; they receive a month's notice if turned away, and live in the hotels; but as a rule, employers do not seem to have any conscience about barmaids. The public ignore them altogether, if we except the hangers-on, who pester them with inane compliments, and the fast men, who decoy them to their ruin.

An attempt has been made by the Young Women's Christian Association to help barmaids, and Miss Gough, the secretary of the Restaurant

Branch, is in communication with many of them. Morley Rooms, 14, John Street, Bedford Row, W.C., has been opened as a centre for those barmaids who care to use it ; and we give an account of a barmaids' "at home" there, witnessed by a Commissioner.

But the Young Women's Christian Association cannot attack the evils from which these girls are suffering—namely, long hours, bad accommodation, low wages, and an excessive allowance of spirits.

The Society is afraid to interfere between employées and employers, because they are dependent on the latter to a great extent, and feel, if the doors were closed upon them, they could not do the work they are doing at present. They are evangelists, not economists. However, they feel much sympathy for the workers—in fact, one of them actually said the other day : "The present state of things is *almost* enough to make one a Socialist."

The Young Women's Christian Association only touches the fringe of the class at the bar. Our Commissioner says that when she arrived at Morley Rooms she found about thirty neatly-dressed young women playing at "coach," and Miss Gough looking on with great satisfaction.

The drawing-rooms they were in had beautifully decorated doors, the work of Mrs. Watts, the wife of the artist. Other ladies had helped to decorate the place, and the rooms were full of pictures, books, and games. One young woman was playing a piano, and the rest were romping in a dignified fashion. The next game was unique. Some newspapers were fastened inside an open doorway, and two holes having been cut large enough to show a pair of eyes, one of the company went behind the newspapers, and the others tried to guess whose eyes were exhibited.

Then some little musicians arrived, and the girls listened to an amateur concert. Downstairs were tables covered with fruit and cakes, tea and coffee, ready for the girls who came pouring in from their work. Miss Gough was in request everywhere; every one wanted to have a word with the hostess.

Morley Rooms, 14, John Street, Bedford Row, W.C., are open to members and friends of the Restaurant Branch of the Young Women's Christian Association for conversation, reading, music, and rest; members and non-members can also be accommodated with lodging and board at moderate prices.

CHAPTER XX.

EAST END TAILORESSES.

THERE is just now, all up and down the social scale, a *furore* for social facts.

A noble lord, who shall be nameless, created quite a sensation last season in a West End drawing-room.

"Only think," he said, "I've actually seen a woman making a match-box!"

The people who collect social facts may be divided into three classes:—

1. The notoriety-seeker, who makes capital by satisfying the curiosity of the public. If any man or woman wishes to become a celebrity (*i.e.*, to be talked about) he or she has only to take up some social question. It is the cheapest sort of advertisement.

2. The economist, who collects and classifies, with the view to founding a true science of economics.

3. The humanitarian, who studies the condition of his fellow-men in order to help them.

The inquiry into sweating is more advanced than any other social inquiry at present, so the three kinds of collectors have come under our notice, and we must give them a passing word.

The notoriety-seeker will be best seen in the following illustration :—

A Commissioner visited a man who was a sweater, and who now sweats himself, who is well known in connection with sweating. This individual was discovered, in a *negligé* costume, sitting on the counter of a small shop, surrounded by herrings, pickles, and other savoury articles. None, he said, knew so much about sweating as himself, but he was not going to be pumped. He had editors at his command, and gentlemen stepping out of carriages at his door; he had promised to take a certain nobleman into some of the sweating dens; but he would do nothing for the classes. He cared for the people; he worked for them; he did not believe in the classes. Besides, he had no time, for he was sweating all day and writing all night.

Imagine, then, how surprised the Commissioner was to see this individual a few days later enjoying a first-rate dinner in a first-rate restaurant, patronised solely by "the classes!"

We would advise the above-mentioned nobleman to take his little son to visit the sweaters

They are proverbially bad-tempered, and little Lord —— has discovered an excellent cure for temper.

Not long ago, at lunch, he suddenly began to gulp, to grow red in the face. Frightened footmen and anxious parents rushed to his assistance.

"I've done it!" he said, with great satisfaction, after he had finished.

"What have you done?" inquired his mother.

"I've swallowed my temper."

The economist is of quite recent growth. A number of men and women, belonging to what are called "the educated classes," are convinced that we have as yet no foundation for a true science of economics. They look upon our present political economists as empiricists, and they desire to collect and classify social facts before attempting to build up a science of economics. As yet they move hither and thither, studying different trades, tabulating the inhabitants of various localities; but they talk of founding a society in order that their work may not overlap. It is very doubtful if they will ever get really accurate information without State assistance. They rather overrate the value of their work, because it is the first attempt in this direction to be accurate; and they use the slang of a trade with great effect upon the uninitiated.

It is amusing to find words such as "slop," "bespoke," etc., treated like scientific terms agreed upon by scientists. They have a curious love of hoarding information. Instead of feeling that the things they are studying need no special talent to be studied, they act just like scholars who bore into dead languages. They snarl at humanitarians much as scholars snarl at their foreign brethren.

The humanitarian is the easiest of the three to work with. He will sit up all night in order to give information, if he is convinced that he burns the midnight oil to a good purpose; he will walk a dozen miles to get an apt illustration, if he thinks by so doing he can help on the cause in which he is so deeply interested. But he has fads; and he is not just to the economist. He thinks the economist has no heart because he does not understand the scientific temperament, and he resents the way in which the economist scoffs at him as a sentimentalist.

"Do you think any good will be done by this inquiry into sweating?" we have asked again and again.

The answer of the sweater and the sweated is the same:

"No; the evidence has been so contradictory."

"You might as well set me to give an opinion

on politics as them lords to give an opinion on sweating," a woman said with supreme contempt. "Why, one of them actually thought we used machines as finishers; he didn't seem to understand if we'd machines we'd be machinists."

It must be explained here that trousers and vests—*i.e.*, waistcoats—are made by two sets of people, machinists and finishers. Women do not make coats—they help the men to finish coats; but the "slop" (lowest class of work) coat trade is entirely in the hands of Jewish tailors.

Mr. Schloss says in his articles on Sweating in *The Fortnightly Review*, December, 1887: "With a coat, style—'form,' as it is called in the trade—is of the first importance; and a coat, if it is to possess 'form,' and so command a ready sale, must of necessity be one in the making of which male labour has largely preponderated. Female labour has always been found fatally deficient in 'form.'"

In the sweaters' "blackholes of industry" one woman may be found working with eight or ten men, finishing coats. The Jewish tailors prefer Gentile women as finishers, because they will work on the Hebrew Sabbath, and they will, as a rule, take lower wages than Jewesses.

Mr. Lakeman, H.M. senior Metropolitan Inspector of Factories, says of the sweaters' dens in East London: "No greater squalor in houses can be seen; no more unhealthy workshops can be found."

The following is Mr. Schloss's account of such a house:—"Directing our steps through the narrow passage of a four-storied tenement dwelling of average size, we find ourselves in a yard which, though never spacious, was formerly of sufficient proportions to supply a reasonable amount of back ventilation. But a few years ago there was erected upon a large portion of this area a three-storied building, each floor of which is a work-room, and is connected with the tenement house we have just quitted by a narrow bridge. Examining what little is left of the original yard, we find that the uneven pavement is studded with pools of stagnant water, while the numerous cracks in the flagstones are filled with noxious rubbish. This area is supposed to be drained by a bell-trap, which, since its cover—as is usual with these unserviceable inventions—has long since disappeared, permits the sewer-gas to escape unchecked from the drain below. The dust-bin stands immediately under the windows of the ground-floor workshop, which, however—perhaps to avoid the stench from the bin, but certainly with the result of rendering ventilation of the interior impracticable—are carefully constructed in such a manner that it is impossible to open them. The lid of the bin is thrown back at right angles to its proper place, so as not to interfere with the exhalations which proceed from a huge pile of refuse. . . . Finding that the ground-floor workshop is to-day without a tenant, we re-enter the house, and having ascended the cramped staircase, reach the stone-flagged bridge leading to the workroom on the floor above. From this gangway the light is all excluded by a high hoarding on both sides—a style of architecture which has been adopted with the view of preventing the tenants of the upper floors from casting forth rubbish from this convenient elevation on to the pavement below. . . . The workshop on the first floor we find in possession of a cabinet-making sweater, who employs from four to fifteen men, according to the orders which he may have on hand ; while the sweater in the fur trade, on the second story, has invited from five to nine workers to enjoy with him the stifling fumes of his coke fire. The tenement house, to which these workshops form an appendix, affords accommodation (the limited character of which may be imagined) for nineteen individuals, belonging to six different families, while its ground floor is used as a butcher's shop."

In a house like this we find the sweater's den,

about which we have heard so much lately. We will describe one of the worst. The room, twelve feet square, held ten people—the sweater, eight men, and one girl. The window-panes were nearly all broken, and filled up with paper or canvas. The gas was burning, also a large coke fire. There was no ventilation whatsoever, and the men were covered with sweat, although they had on the veriest apologies for clothes. The girl wore an old ragged dress, open at the chest. Her forehead was studded with perspiration, and her hair was wet. The men had tins of beer beside their machines, and a large mug of beer stood on the pressers' table. All the men were Jews, but the girl was a Gentile.

Such rooms are found chiefly in Spitalfields, Whitechapel, and the Jewish ghetto.

But the greater number of East End tailoresses make trousers and vests at home ; comparatively few are found working in " the blackholes of industry." Their number is said to be 25,000, and they are mostly Gentiles, living in Stepney, Bow, and Shoreditch.

It is extremely difficult to get accurate information about the hours of work and the payment of these East End tailoresses. The following figures have been most kindly supplied by an excellent authority :—

Lowest Class of Trousers.—6*d.* per pair paid to sweater by manufacturer; 1¾*d.* or 2*d.* per pair paid by sweater to machinist; 2½*d.* per pair paid by sweater to finisher. Profit of sweater 1½*d.*

Second Class of Trousers.—9*d.* per pair paid to sweater by manufacturer; 2¾*d.* per pair paid by sweater to machinist; 3¾*d.* per pair paid by sweater to finisher, including pressing. Profit of sweater 2½*d.*

Third Class of Trousers.—1*s.* 2*d.* per pair paid to sweater by manufacturer; 3¾*d.* per pair paid by sweater to machinist; 4*d.* per pair, with extra 1*d.* for pressing, paid by sweater to finisher. Profit of sweater 5¼*d.*

Vests or Waistcoats.—These are made right out by one woman.—6*d.* per vest paid to sweater by manufacturer; 4½*d.* per vest paid by sweater to tailoress. Profit of sweater 1½*d.*

9*d.* per vest paid to sweater by manufacturer; 7*d.* per vest paid by sweater to tailoress. Profit of sweater 2*d.*

1*s.* per vest paid to sweater by manufacturer; 9*d.* per vest paid by sweater to tailoress. Profit of sweater 3*d.*

Juvenile Suits in Two Garments.—6*d.* per suit paid to sweater; 1¾*d.* per suit paid by sweater to machinist; 2¾*d.* per suit paid by sweater to finisher. Profit of sweater 1½*d.*

These figures give the payment per garment; but, with the machinists, money must be deducted for the hire of the machine, soap, thread, and firing. Singer's machines cost 2*s.* 6*d.* per week, and although machines can be hired at lower prices, they do not work well under 2*s.* or 1*s.* 6*d.* per week. These machines are often forfeited during slack times, and the women find it difficult to buy them by weekly instalments. Finishers provide their own cotton, gimp, silk, irons, press-cloths, firing, and oil, for they get the work late, and sit up at night. Both machinists and finishers are often kept hours waiting for their work in the sweaters' shops, and as seats are seldom provided, they find the loads heavy to carry home after hours spent standing. The hours they work vary of course, but it has been calculated that their work lasts sixteen or seventeen hours a day when they can get employment, and is paid at the rate of little more than *a penny an hour.* Slack seasons are from the second week of December to the first week in February, also for two weeks after Whitsuntide and three weeks after the August Bank Holiday. The slackest season is just about Christmas.

We do not intend to discuss the sweating system; the public has heard too much already about it. We merely wish to point out that there are about 25,000 East End tailoresses working sixteen or seventeen hours a day, at the rate of about 1*d.* per hour, when they can get employment. Making trousers and vests is a home industry; but the rooms of the workers are not much better than the dens of the sweaters.

The sweater works hard himself. It is the giver-out who makes the greatest profit. The foremen and passers, or givers-out, have not been sufficiently noticed. The sweaters could afford to pay their workers better if they were not obliged to tip these men; but these men will not give the sweaters work until they have taken a heavy toll, which ultimately comes out of the workers' pockets.

We have not space to notice the Workwomen's Co-operative Association, Limited, but it is making a profit while it gives good wages. It has raised the pay of the tailoresses all round the district, and is doing away, to some extent, with the evils connected with the sweating system, namely, "excessive lowness of wages, unduly prolonged hours of labour, irregularity of employment, and unhealthy workshops."

CHAPTER XXI.

LAUNDRESSES—STRIKERS—UPHOLSTERESSES.

A LARGE number of girls and women work as laundresses in the central metropolitan districts. They prepare factory goods for the market—more especially collars and cuffs. Their work is called "dressing." When a laundry department is attached to the factory where the goods are made, the pay is fair; but when the work is given out, laundresses do not get very much, because many people compete for the work, and the middle-man, or middle-woman, takes the profit. Laundresses are generally divided into four classes—washers, ironers, collar-ironers, and learners. All four classes work, as a rule, four or five days a week, from 9 a.m. to 8 p.m., with three-quarters of an hour for dinner and half an hour for tea. The following is their scale of payment: Washers, 2*s.* 6*d.* to 2*s.* 8*d.* per day; ironers, 3*s.* 6*d.* to 4*s.* per day, piece-work; collar-ironers, 3*s.* 6*d.* to 5*s.* per day, piece-work;

learners, 1*s.* a day for three months, then 3*d.* a day extra for three months up to 2*s.* 6*d.*

They are said to take "good money;" but considering the nature of their work, and the fact that they generally live far away from the laundries, their pay is not much. Few people realise what severe labour it is to "dress" the collars and cuffs sold in the shops—how much "elbow grease" it needs to give them a shiny appearance. Gas-irons, which must be lifted constantly to the gas, and little curled irons, which must be twisted in and out, are more exhausting than the "goose," or heavy iron, and all these require that the work should be done standing. *A laundress stands all day*, with the exception of her dinner-hour and the half-hour allowed for tea, and the heat of the room she works in makes her work doubly trying, for windows cannot be opened on account of London smuts. Fans are arranged in the centre of the rooms; nevertheless the atmosphere is generally such that the girls faint again and again, owing to the heat and the long hours they spend on their feet. It is no uncommon thing to hear that a laundress has gone into what her friends call "a consumption," for in the winter, when she leaves the hot laundry and goes into the street, the sudden change of air affects her chest. In the laundry she wears a thin cotton dress, loose at the neck; her face and arms are moist with perspiration, and her hair is dank. Leaving this place, she throws on an old coat, and hurries out to "cool herself." She has, perhaps, "an awful backache;" so she sits down for a few minutes to rest before she trudges off to her home, which is a mile or two away from the City. In this way many a girl meets her death, and when she drops out of the ranks another girl begins to dress the linen; and so the game goes on, without a thought being given by the public to the poor, overworked laundress.

Many of these "dressing" laundries are below the street. Into some one descends by a flight of at least twenty steps; and when there one thinks of the Black Hole of Calcutta while watching the girls at work. Long rows of young women on either side of narrow tables attract one's attention first, and then one sees the gas flaring above the bent heads, while every minute a bare arm is raised to light a gas-iron or to lift a goose. Little girls in short petticoats, with hair down their backs—learners—supply the ironers with work, count the dressed goods, and run errands. And all this is done in a stifling atmosphere, with wafts of heavy, steam-laden air from the fans in the centre of the room, and draughts from open doors leading upstairs into the factory or the street. Few people are more to be pitied than young laundresses. When older they grow accustomed to the work; but the habit of taking in mere children as learners is sad to witness. The older women complain bitterly about these children, more especially in large steam laundries, where soiled linen is washed, because there children can feed the big machines, and do work which was formerly done by skilled laundresses.

In the steam laundries it is no uncommon thing to find 200 or 300 women, girls, and children working from 7 a.m. to 7 p.m., and often until 10 p.m. The workers are divided in these laundries into sorters, markers, packers ironers, and forewomen or superintendents. The pay varies a little in different places, and it is nearly all piece-work; but the following table is fairly correct for all the large soiled linen laundries in the different metropolitan districts:—

Sorters, 1*s.* 6*d.* per day; overtime, $1\frac{1}{2}$*d.* per hour. Markers and packers, 1*s.* 9*d.*, 2*s.*, and 2*s.* 6*d* per day; overtime, $1\frac{3}{4}$*d.*, 2*d.*, and 3*d.* per hour. Ironers, 3*s.* 6*d.* per day; overtime, 4*d.* per hour Forewomen, 5*s.* per day; overtime, $5\frac{1}{2}$*d.* or 6*d* per hour.

Some of these laundries have sick funds for the employées, which entitle the workers to 1*s.* per day during illness, and a doctor's visits, on payment of 2*d.* per week. On the whole, great care is taken to guard the machinery; and after careful investigation we find that very few accidents occur that are not due to the careless behaviour of the workers, who grow so accustomed to the machines that they treat them without sufficient respect, and consequently get punished.

It is curious that in these steam laundries both managers and forewomen complain of the girls sent to them by clergymen and societies. Such girls do not work nearly as well as those who feel that they have nothing to fall back upon but their club; no one to bolster them up if they prove incompetent. We realise in these factories that charity is out of date, and that all the girls want is to be taught to help themselves. They are ripe for a trades union, more especially as they feel the prick of the capitalist's last weapon; namely, the child-labour which he is calling in to lessen their numbers and lower their wages.

STRIKERS.

It may be well to notice here the little errand-girls—*alias* strikers, *alias* matchers, *alias* trotters—who are now employed in the place of learners or apprentices. We find them everywhere, and they have not as yet attracted the attention of the public. We spoke some time ago about the slaveys who work in different houses—mind babies, run errands, and wash up—for *2s. 6d.* a week and tea, who sleep at home, and are generally called day-maids. Many of these slaveys would become regular servants if they had clothes to enter domestic service; but possessing no change of garments and only one very bad pair of boots, they look out for small places among their neighbours when the Board school sets them free to earn their own living, or they apply for situations as errand-girls in places of business.

No matter where you go in the poorer parts of London, you may see advertisements in private windows, on shop doors, or on street walls, for strikers, trotters, and matchers; namely, little errand-girls. Such girls are generally supposed to do domestic work, to run errands, to wait on workrooms, and to perform the easiest parts of whatever employment is carried on by their master or mistress. They match materials for dressmakers; they sweep rooms and make tea for tailors; they are, in fact, the slaveys of people in business. West End workrooms have such errand-girls attached to them, girls of rather a superior position; and East End sweating dens find them necessary. These girls, if quick, pick up a smattering of whatever is going on, and are soon able to take the place of learners or apprentices. Employers find them cheap, and in spite of remonstrances on the part of trained workers, the little girls slip into the position of those who used to "be taught a living." Sometimes they palm themselves off as trained workers after a year or six months spent as errand-girls.

Many sink thus into the lowest depths of misery and sin, being taken on by employers of the worst class to do any sort of work at any rate of payment. Some gradually push their way forward, and end by taking high-class wages; but they have no status as trotters, strikers, etc., and they are the prey of unscrupulous employers, who use them without giving them a proper training. All over London one hears complaints about those poor little slaveys; and the workers agree that the employers ought not to employ them instead of apprentices.

UPHOLSTERESSES.

The upholsteress is doomed; her trade is dying, and before long she will have vanished. Her work is to help men dress or furnish houses; to make curtains, carpets, blinds, mattresses, etc.

Machinery now does the work which was formerly done by women, and, as an upholsteress said lately, "Girls are employed as finishers, and do the machine work in the place of women, at a rate of wages insufficient for their support, unless assisted by parents and friends."

This woman has been working at the trade for many years. She remembers the day when the work was such that in many places the employées worked all night; but now she says the slack season lasts from November to March, with a little rush before Christmas, and that very few hands are wanted in the largest places of business.

The greater number of upholsteresses work by the day, and earn in the West End from 15*s.* to 17*s.* a week, in the Central Metropolitan district from 12*s.* to 14*s.* a week, and in some cases from 18*s.* to 20*s.* a week for the best furniture.

In no trade does one hear more bitter complaints against child-labour than among the upholsteresses. They look with horror and disgust on the little girls from the Board schools who begin with 3*s.* or 4*s.* a week, and press on to the front before they become young women

It would be well to notice here the statement quoted above, namely, that many girls are engaged at a rate of wages insufficient for their support unless assisted by parents or friends.

Employers can scarcely be blamed for preferring girls who are not self-dependent. There are plenty of girls in the labour-market whose parents cannot afford to keep them at home doing nothing, but who can give them pocket-money—namely, enough to buy clothes and pay for their locomotion. Employers naturally seek out such girls, for they do not feel so morally bound to them; they know in slack times that such girls have homes to go to, and that they need not give such girls high wages. Of course, all this is very hard on the self-dependent girls; but, alas! to her that hath shall be given, and from her that hath not shall be taken away. It is difficult to suggest a remedy. Every day more girls are forced to compete in the labour market, owing to the difficulty which men find in getting work, and employers are sure to prefer girls who have a little home assistance to those who are self-dependent. The evil lies very deep, and nothing can be done while the market is so overcrowded.

At present many absurd mistakes are made as to the meaning of an employer's words when he says, "I want girls who are not self-dependent." Guardians and philanthropists rise up in arms when they hear this statement; but the fact that employers can get girls who are partially supported by their relations throws a cold, calm light on this remonstrance, and they begin to realise that no harm is meant—nothing but that the employer wants to buy his labour-force in the cheapest possible market.

CHAPTER XXII.

SEMPSTRESSES—WEST END TAILORESSES.

WHAT is a sempstress?

Before Mr. Walter Besant called attention to working girls by his creation of Melenda, the sempstress was the only female worker who interested the public. Poets wrote about her, and she was quoted as a person much to be pitied, working in a garret, and living on next to nothing.

So far as we can make out, she is Jill of all trades and mistress of none. Dressmakers abuse her for taking work out of their hands, and upholsteresses say that she intrudes where she is not wanted. We shall class her here as the maker of underclothing; not only as an unskilled hand in her own home, but as a skilled machinist working for her daily bread in metropolitan factories.

The woman who makes shirts or waistcoats for men calls herself a sempstress, and certainly the women who work at collars and cuffs for ladies and gentlemen are sempstresses ; while the same name is given to the maker of babies' robes and such garments ! But the large number of women engaged in making underclothing are all we mean to notice here under the title of "sempstresses."

Mr. Lakeman, H.M. Chief Inspector, tells us in his last report on the "Social Condition of Female Operatives in the Factories and Workshops of the Central Metropolitan District," that the trade of female underclothing includes the manufacturing of sundry articles ; and as it is a light and clean business, girls of a superior class are found at work, evidently the daughters of parents who set them good examples.

The best quality carries as much as 25 per cent. of cost of article in manufacturing, and quickest machine hands earn 20*s.* to 22*s.* per week ; but hand-workers, who must be neat sewers, range from 12*s.* to 17*s.*, piecework. The seasons do not affect this industry, and the workers can generally reckon on steady, continuous employment, whereby the class mentioned are drawn to it. The price of labour has decreased here owing to the development of domestic workshops, wherein cheap goods are made, and where no restriction on labour exists.

The sewing machine, whilst cheapening the

cost of production, has increased the wage of operative machine hands, but hand-workers remain much under the old system of payment.

Mr. Lakeman gives the wages of learners in this trade at 2*s*. 6*d*. per week, young hands at 5*s*. to 10*s*. per week, experienced workers at 15*s*. per week, and extra clever workers at 20*s*. to 22*s*. per week.

Here, again, we find the wives and daughters of clerks and tradesmen competing *sub rosa* for work which can be done at home, underselling their poorer sisters.

We have been told by at least half-a-dozen employers that ladies send their servants to fetch this work and carry it back, and that ladies will undertake it at lower prices than are given to ordinary sempstresses.

Miss Clementina Black, the excellent secretary of the Women's Trades Union and Provident League, has written an interesting article on sempstresses in the *Women's World* entitled "Something about Needlewomen."

She takes for her text the factory of Messrs. Stapley & Smith, in London Wall and Fore Street. She tells us that the workrooms there are above the average, and says of the workers :—

"As we go round and watch the work being done, we perceive that these girls can do things almost miraculous. Children's frocks and pinafores are being made—little delicate garments with tiny tucks and lace edgings, and minute runners of fine tape in the top hem. And these tape-runners the girls do not slip in with a bodkin; no, they like to go a quicker way: they stitch the hem, which is perhaps a quarter of an inch wide, with the tape in it. To do that and never fix it is a feat indeed. One girl I saw stitching on lace; the lace was frilled, and she frilled it with her fingers as she stitched. Nothing is tacked, and yet the exactitude and delicacy of the work are faultless. . . . And this work is done with very great rapidity. The whizz of the machines seems deafening to a newcomer; but the workers talk through it with no raising of the voice. One corner of the room is noisiest of all; it is the corner where the button-hole machines stand. The button-hole is made in a fraction of a minute; and when a garment has all its button-holes made, it is tossed to a young girl at a table to cut, for the machine does not cut. She has a little instrument with a blade precisely the right length, and laying the garment on the table, makes incision after incision. There is, of course, a certain danger of cutting the sewn edge, but with the proper instrument this danger is slight. Another young girl takes the garment, gives it a sharp shake, lays it flat on the deal table, and folds it in the twinkling of an eye.

"And now, what is the pay of these accomplished machinists? Their working hours in this house are from half-past eight to six, with an hour for dinner and half an hour for tea. On Saturdays they stop at one. No overtime is allowed; great care is taken never to keep them waiting unoccupied; and the work is absolutely constant, because, when the demand is slack, stock can be accumulated to meet its recurrence. . . . I was allowed to look into any I pleased of the pile of wages-books. I found that the average earnings were about 15*s.* a week: the best workers would make £1; while the very worst among them averaged scarcely 8*s.* or 9*s.* . . . Button-holers make more—as much perhaps as 23*s.* a week, which is reckoned opulence for a working woman. . . . And these, remember, are the highest wages earned under the most favourable circumstances. . . . For every woman working in the light, clean, and airy rooms of Messrs. Stapley & Smith, there are ten working with insufficient space, imperfect sanitary arrangements, and the harassing of a constant sense of unjust treatment; and of these ten, not five, perhaps, will earn, on a yearly average, more than 10*s.* a week, even though they work nine or ten hours a day."

West End Tailoresses.

We have had a good deal of conversation about these women with a man who has collected information for what he called "The Lords' Committee," about the foreign tailors in Soho and the neighbourhood of Regent Street. Fifteen years ago the foreigners congregated in two or three streets; now they are spreading, and are taking the work out of the hands of Englishmen, although they give employment to large numbers of Englishwomen. They are chiefly Swedes. They work harder and live cheaper than our own countrymen, and they are more popular with employers, because they will do work at any hour, and sit up night after night to get it finished. Some of these foreign tailors live in wretched houses, and in order to find their workrooms it is necessary to climb up filthy staircases; but the workrooms are, as a rule, large and well ventilated. A great deal of work is done on Sunday, and overtime is much practised. The workers, however, are well paid, and the work is regular.

Here, as in the East End, we find women helping to make coats, basting, sewing on buttons, putting in lining, and making button holes. Good machinists earn from 20*s.* to 28*s.* a week, and some take as much as 30*s.* Trousers are generally made in the workshops; but a good deal of slop work is done at home, and not a little of the best work is taken home to finish. This is piece-work, and paid as follows:—plain trousers, 1*s.* 3*d.*; better, 1*s.* 6*d.*; best, 1*s.* 9*d.* per pair. A woman can make three pairs of plain trousers in a day if she is a quick worker, and two pairs of better or best trousers. These she makes by herself, with no assistance from the tailor further than the pressing and the cutting out. Waistcoats are generally fetched by the workers straight from the shops, and paid at the rate of 2*s.* 6*d.*, 3*s.* 6*d.*, and 4*s.* 6*d.* per vest. A good worker can make two waistcoats in a day, but she must work hard to do this, especially if she makes first-class waistcoats. Few West End tailoresses earn less than £1 a week, and some earn 30*s.* We have met with several who earn as much as 36*s.* The men complain that the women and the foreigners are taking all the trade; but as women will never be able to make a coat right out, and the Swedes are now calling in young men of their own nation to take the place of Englishwomen, we may expect to see the whole of the West End tailoring in the hands of foreigners before the end of the century.

Errand-girls, or strikers, fetch the work and carry it back to the shops. Some people say that these girls are allowed a percentage on the work they bring to their employers, and that consequently the fast girls make great profits. But we have not been able to trace a single case of this. Neither have we seen the workrooms in which the strikers are said to live by day and sleep by night, together with their master and mistress. Strikers earn 5*s.* a week, and "pick up" the business.

The worst workroom that has come under our notice is built out of a house and reached by a ladder. This room is attached to a tumble-down house at the back of Regent Street. Passing through a court, and mounting the ladder, we came into a room about eight feet by ten feet, without any window. A large table filled the place, having space at the further end for a woman who was "finishing," and the little striker who was waiting for orders. On the table squatted four tailors, busy with work for a well-known house. The heat was terrific, for a large fire burnt at the back of the woman who was finishing, and the door could not be left open on account of the draught. Presently a smartly-dressed young man came in with a black bag, out of which he produced "Lord ——'s coat," which must be done, he said, at once.

He came from a house which professes to have all its work done on the premises ; and having emptied the contents of his bag, he departed, with instructions that the coat should be sent home without fail the following morning. If the owner of the coat could see the den in which his garment was made he might feel a little uncomfortable, for the place was very dirty, and not free from vermin. The striker was sent to fetch some beer, as the men said that they would be obliged to work late. They could not stretch their legs without going down the ladder, and when the presser wanted to use his irons, the finisher was obliged to move away, for the place was so crowded. They were all making good money, they said, and seemed quite contented.

We have heard no complaints about work among West End tailoresses, but they strongly object to the legislation which forbids them to work the same hours as men, and they say that the Factory Act is "very hard on us poor women."

CHAPTER XXIII.

BOOT AND SHOE MAKERS.

THE annual output of boots and shoes from the factories of the United Kingdom is said to be no less than one hundred millions of pairs.

It is impossible to say how many pairs are made in London, but the following are the principal places in which boots and shoes are made. We give them in the order of their importance:—London, Leicester, Northampton, Bristol, Leeds, Norwich, and Stafford.

In all these places girls and women are largely employed, their work being in connection with the tops or uppers of the boots and shoes. It is estimated that the wages paid to females in this trade amount to about five million pounds sterling annually.

The women's and children's boot and shoe trade has developed within the last ten years throughout Hackney, Bethnal Green, and Spitalfields, both in large manufactories and small workshops; and here, also, we find women and girls employed chiefly in making the tops or uppers, although some women can last and click quite as well as men.

It may be wise to explain how a boot is built. The clicker cuts out the tops and uppers; and these uppers are given to women, who make them by a process we will describe later on. When the uppers are finished; the laster puts on the soles and heels by foot or power machine. The finisher adapts the completed or built-up articles to the market. Thus it will be seen that a boot or shoe is built up by four people: (1) the clicker or cutter-out; (2) the upper sewers: these are divided again into fitters and machinists; (3) the laster; and (4) the finisher. Sometimes a fifth person is employed, namely, a sole-sewer; but pegged boots require no sole-sewing.

It is impossible for any one to understand boot-building who has not seen boots in the hands of the clickers, lasters, and others; and probably very few of our readers will care to study the subject. It is extremely complicated, and at the same time most interesting. No two pairs of boots are exactly the same; each pair possesses an individuality of its own, although neither name nor number is given to it. That this is true of the one hundred million pairs of boots annually manufactured, any employer of labour can bear witness.

At one time all the best ladies' shoes were made in France, but now the English wholesale manufacturer can produce the very finest shoes at lower prices than the French shoemakers ask; and although German and Swiss manufacturers press our manufacturers hard, the bulk of the trade has fallen into the hands of English bootmakers.

The editor of *The Shoe and Leather Record* says: "The factory system and the introduction of machinery is revolutionising all the old handicrafts, and boots and shoes are nowadays produced chiefly by manufacturers, who supply the retail shops."

He proceeds to tell us a secret. "Even the bootmaker," he says, "who takes your measure for a pair of boots, presumably to make himself, hands over the order to the manufacturer, who supplies him with his ordinary stock." This being the case, it is useless for people to go through the farce of being measured for boots; they may as well accept "our very best article made by ourselves," with good grace.

The East End trade must be dealt with, so far as women are concerned, in two parts: (1) the work done in manufactories; (2) the work done in small workshops, or the houses of women who employ labour at home.

One of the best manufactories is that of Mr. John Branch, in the Bethnal Green Road. Mr. John Branch takes great interest in his female hands, and the arrangements made for their comfort contrast favourably with other factories. The girls are kept on all the year round; they work in a large, airy room, have full time allowed for meals, and tea provided on the premises.

The girls make the tops or uppers of boots and shoes, and are divided into machinists and fitters. The machinists work by the hour, the fitters do piece-work.

According to Mr. John Branch, machinists take, as a rule, about 14*s.* a week, and fitters about 15*s.* a week, in manufactories. Of course, these wages mean that "findings," namely, silk, thread, needles, oil, etc., are given to the machinists by the employers. When girls provide their own "findings," their gross earnings are from 12*s.* to 25*s.* a week.

A machinist employed on a class of work in which silk is used, has to pay for about 12*s.* or 14*s.* worth of silk, etc., before she has 25*s.* for herself; and, generally speaking, the silk has to be purchased from the employer, he being ultimately responsible for the quality used in the boots.

The system of making girls pay for their "findings" is said to work well, as it teaches them to be careful; but whether they pay or not, it will be found that the wages in East End factories average about 14*s.* a week for machinists and 15*s.* a week for fitters. The work needs considerable training, so it is not overrun with unskilled labour, like many other businesses; and a good fitter can command her price anywhere, if work is not very slack. It is much more difficult to fit than to do the machining.

Mr. Lakeman, H.M. Inspector, gives the following rates of payment in manufactories, but he says nothing about "findings:"—

First year, 3*s.* per week; second year, 4*s.*; third year, 5*s.*; then 10*s.* to 12*s.*; very best machine hands 15*s.* to 20*s.* On the whole, we may say that women and girls engaged in making the uppers of boots and shoes are well paid in manufactories. Of course, few workrooms are like those which Mr. John Branch provides for his hands; but the work is clean, and attracts a superior class of young women. The deafening noise of the machines renders it difficult to study the work of building uppers; and the fact that each upper is composed of six or more parts, and passes through the hands of eight or ten women, is confusing.

Each upper has (1) two quarters, (2) button-piece, (3) golosh, (4) vamp, (5) toe-cap, (6) top-band, (7) five pieces of lining. The golosh and toe-cap are sometimes omitted. Each upper passes through the following hands:—(1) lining-maker, (2) closer, (3) seam-stitcher, (4) fitter, (5) scollop stitcher, (6) button-hole worker, (7) button-hole finisher, (8) buttoning and covering, (9) vamping, (10) sewing up. The most difficult part of the work is to fit the lining to the leather and paste it. Large numbers of boots and shoes are sent to the Colonies, so the paste contains insect powder, which keeps the flour from fermenting. This paste is used to fix the lining and leather together before the upper goes to the machinist, and everything must be done with the greatest nicety. The seams are not allowed to vary by as much as the thirty-second part of an inch. If everything is not absolutely accurate the upper will not fit the last. And as the upper sometimes contains twenty parts, readers may imagine that the work requires both skill and patience.

We now pass on to the work which is done in small workshops and the homes of women Many manufacturers merely cut out the materials and give the work to sweaters. Mr. Lakeman says: "The sweating system is adopted here quite as much as is done in the tailoring trade. Women who are known to be good workers can get material whereon to employ as many hands as their homes can accommodate, and who are paid a like price to the workshop hands of the manufacturer; or the man who is known gets a supply of leather from a manufacturer, who will make special terms with him, and manage to keep him bound by monetary obligations as long as he suits him. This man is an agent, a sweater, who may have several women, employing from eight to twelve hands, working for him at their homes."

We have visited some of these sweaters, and many of the women who employ girls in their rooms or wooden shanties at the backs of their houses. After carefully examining wage books, we have come to the conclusion that both sweaters and women are scarcely better off than the hands themselves. Low-class boots and shoes are sold for little more than the cost of the soles and the leather, and these are the goods that find their way to such people.

We visited a sweater who had refused an order for 1,500 pairs of boots because his profit on them would only be *6d.* in the £; little enough, considering his horse and cart, premises for storing goods, and his own labour. Such men work harder than the people they employ, and often take orders by which they gain nothing, because they are afraid of losing their best hands. It is the same with the women who employ girls at home. The following authentic case will show what distress goes on among the women who take the work home from the manufactories :—

Mrs. —— was charged last June at the —— police-court with stealing forty pairs of uppers. She said : "I am a widow with four children ; my oldest boy has just passed the fourth standard, and, as I am placed, I took him away from school and got him a place where he was earning three shillings a week, which would be a great help to me to pay the rent, but the School Board officer has made me send him to school again. I used to be forewoman of a machine-room before I was married, but after that I did machining at home. I had a beautiful home when my husband, who was a saddler, was alive, and at one time I used to earn good money. I have earned as much as 30*s.* a week, but that is years ago. The machine-work is shockingly paid for now ; but as for this charge against me, I am ashamed to talk about it. My name has got into all the papers, and I am ashamed to show myself outside the door. I can't explain to everybody the circumstances."

Here Mrs. —— was greatly agitated with hysterical sobs, which continued more or less throughout the interview.

"Is it true that you machined work at 5*d.* per dozen?"

"Yes, it is quite true. They were babies' patent leather shoes, sateen-lined, with front springs. I had to put on five buttons. I employ a fitter; to her I had to pay 2½*d.* per dozen for fitting, and a halfpenny for putting on the buttons. The outlay for cotton and paste would be about another halfpenny for a dozen."

"Out of what is left, I suppose you have to buy needles, oil, and pay for what repairs the machine may require?"

"Yes, certainly; the machine is my own. I bought it on the hire system. I finished paying for it just after my husband died."

"How many of these babies' shoes could you do in a day?"

"The two of us, working from eight to eight, could do six dozens: but I often work from five or six in the morning to ten or eleven o'clock at night. I used to have some work for which I was paid 8*d.* per dozen; they were mock kid shoes, black leather lined, turned-in linings. For these I had to pay 4*d.* for fitting and another 1*d.* for staying; that would leave me 3*d.* for machining and cotton. If I worked very hard I could do four dozen of these in a day. The work at 1*s.* a dozen were mock kid balmorals, with leather top-bands and leather inside facings. For these I had to pay 6*d.* for fitting, and 1*d.* for staying, and it would cost me about 3½*d.* a day for cotton. We had to skive all the top-bands before we could turn them in. This was cruel work for the money. We could not do more than three dozen a day, if we worked ever so hard. I could earn more on the babies' work. Then, besides, they are so shocking particular. They turn every upper inside out, and for every little fault the work is returned."

"'Are you an experienced machinist?"

"Yes; I have been at it since I was a little girl, and was forewoman at Mr. —— till I was married. Some machinists earn good money, even at these prices, but the way they do it is by employing learners, who work three months for nothing, and then they go elsewhere as improvers, and for some part of the work they employ improvers at a few shillings a week. But I can't do that. I could not leave my children to go to shop, so I had to get a woman to do that for me, which used to cost *4d.* for riding every time. She has left my place sometimes at eight o'clock in the morning, and did not get back until half-past twelve."

"How much do you earn a week?"

"If I can earn 10*s.* a week I can manage to do; I have earned 12*s.* or 13*s.* a week sometimes; but I could not tell any one how we manage to live; we have something—that's all I can say. I was well brought up, and like to keep my children decently dressed; but it's very hard, God knows."

It is true that girls who work for women like this earn very little, and toil for many hours.

Some of the rooms they work in are not fit for human habitation, mere dens. Often they are daughters or nieces of women who fetch the work from the sweaters, or straight from the manufacturers.

One room we visited was below the street, dark, filthy beyond description, and full of Singer's machines, some in good order, some out of repair. Six girls worked them, and they would do 45 dozen pairs of uppers in a day; but the work was slack, they said, and they were taking low wages. The paster had only earned 2*s.* 6*d.* the previous week, and the other girls 6*s.* and 8*s.* Work is always slackest about Christmas.

It is quite impossible to say what money these girls take, for the work varies, and the slack seasons are so long that no two girls seem to get the same amount of money. Mr. Lakeman says: "Females are generally paid" (in such places) "by the week, and girls of fourteen are engaged nominally for a year as apprentices, at 2*s.* 6*d.* a week; they are then called table hands, blacking the leather, button-holes, and buttons, helping the fitter, for which they get 7*s.* a week. An ordinary machinist can earn 9*s.* to 10*s.* a week, but one who works on best goods goes up to 12*s.*, 14*s.*, and 15*s.*; a good fitter makes 12*s.* a week, whilst hand workers must be content with 7*s.* or 8*s.* From March to November work is brisk, but for the winter no great provision can be made. The outworkers are very slack, and very badly off. Whatever there is done is generally confined to the factory or the workshop proper."

A great deal of distress is found among these poor people at Christmas time, the most dreary season of the year for such workers. Singer's machines must be forfeited, because the money for them is not forthcoming; and as many have husbands and brothers out of work, few are likely to have "a merry Christmas."

Mr. John Branch, who has given his attention to the sweating question, says the only solution is the employment of a large number of sanitary inspectors, for then the work will be driven into the factories, and home industries will die a natural death. Doubtless readers will hide their heads like ostriches in the sands of good wishes, while the girls who are "out of work" dream of roast beef and plum-pudding. What can be done?

It is a difficult question.

CHAPTER XXIV.

YOUNG WOMEN.

WE propose to take a survey of the articles on Young Women in London. We have noticed the following classes: Flower-girls and street-hawkers; factory-girls and City work-girls; girls engaged in home industries; East and West End tailoresses; East and West End shirtmakers; sempstresses, upholsteresses, and laundresses; servants; barmaids; and the girls engaged in the boot and shoe industry.

It has been impossible to do more than glance at the work and wages of these young women. The subject is very large, and our space is limited. No paper, no individual, can deal with the mass of information which must be obtained, and sifted, before the public can have accurate information about London girls after they leave the Board Schools. But each investigation helps, if it is honest; for others gather up the threads and weave them into more perfect knowledge.

It may interest our readers to know that Mr. Charles Booth, who has done, and is doing, such valuable statistical work in London, has added to his secretaries a lady whose business it will be to inquire into the work and wages of girls in East London.

She will, let us hope, carry on similar investigations in other parts of the Metropolis, and so, at last, we shall have an idea of female labour in London. But it must be borne in mind that such investigations are, at the best, only approximate. We may, in time, get enough facts to build up a science of economics; but we shall never have the truth, for facts change—the truth is not stationary.

"When I want to laugh I read 'Adam Bede,'" remarked a carpenter. "George Eliot's idea of my trade is funnier to me than anything I come across in *Ally Sloper*."

Just as the novelist gives the shadows of men and women more or less distinctly according to his talent for character-painting, so does the investigator give tables of facts more or less accurately. It is all very well for economists to smile because Mr. Walter Besant's inquiry into the work and wages of women has collapsed—to say, "That is what one might expect of a novelist." By his creation of Melenda, Mr.

Besant first called attention to the working girl of London. The artist suggests: the economist merely puts his suggestions into practice.

Our inquiry has taught us that the flower-girl, or street hawker, is the daughter of the casual; often Irish and a Roman Catholic, generally improvident, and the victim of a loafer, who spends her money and refuses to support his children unless she has her "lines," or marriage certificate. We have seen that the factory-girl proper is the daughter of the labouring-man; well paid in first-class factories, but generally a drug in the market, earning from 4*s.* to 8*s.* a week, which money goes into the family pocket. The City work-girl we have found to be the daughter of the skilled artizan; often a stranger to London, where she suffers terribly in slack seasons, and has to seek cheap lodgings, in which companions are met who, being stronger and more skilful, lead her on step by step till the *facile descensus* is complete. The girls engaged in home industries we have discovered in the lowest depths of poverty and distress in the East End districts. Our readers found our statements too much for their feelings, and we were able to help some of the worst cases through their kindness. The plain needle-women, the fur-pullers, the brush-makers, and others we have unearthed in miserable dens, dragging out their lives amid dirt and wretchedness on the pittance given to them by middlemen. Afterwards we had to state on the authority of one who has lived for years among them, that 25,000 East End tailoresses are working fifteen and sixteen hours a day for a penny an hour, when they can get employment; fetching their work from sweaters' shops, where they are kept standing for hours, and then consuming the midnight oil in order that they may earn a few pennies. The West End tailoress, who shines brightly in comparison, had nevertheless a distinct grievance, which was, that the whole of the tailoring trade is rapidly passing into the hands of foreigners, who are calling in young men of their own nation to take the place of Englishwomen. East End shirt-makers have been visited who finish shirts at one farthing each; laundresses who dress linen for shops, upholsteresses and sempstresses, have all come under our notice. Servants *versus* mistresses, and mistresses *versus* servants, occupied a considerable amount of our space; and we pointed out that if the London Board Schools would affiliate themselves with the Metropolitan Association for Befriending Young Servants, the poor little trotters, alias strikers, alias slaveys, might be saved from the clutches of those who now employ them in the place of proper apprentices, to the disadvantage of all trained workers. Our article on barmaids drew attention to those "called to the bar." We told the public that these girls work ten and twelve hours a day at many of the best-known restaurants, receive an allowance of 10*d.* a day for spirits, and sleep below the street in some of the Metropolitan stations. Last of all we spoke of the girls who make the uppers of boots and shoes, and proved to our readers that such workers are not likely to enjoy a very merry Christmas.

We have not space to discuss what can be done to improve the condition of these young women. They are willing to emigrate, and we are told on the best authority that the girls who are a drug here can have work in the Colonies. But while foreigners come in to take their places we can scarcely say that they ought to leave England. The most serious fact we have had to state is that twenty thousand girls have of late years been added to the lists of those who ply the only trade that has no slack times for women; and that many of these are foreigners. That we want more factory inspectors H.M.I. Mr. Lakeman bore witness before the Sweating Commission; and that sanitary inspectors must overhaul the workers in home industries is very evident. We would make one suggestion. Let work be found for the unemployed men, and thus lift from the shoulders of their wives and daughters the burden of bread-winning.

Miss Clementina Black, Secretary of the Women's Trades' Union and Provident League, has given us active help; and we are glad to hear that her work is bearing fruit in the shape of Unions among the shop-assistants, laundresses, and others.

We have also received much sympathy and assistance from the secretaries of the Young Women's Christian Association. These ladies cannot touch the economic question; if they did, employers would quickly close upon them the doors of factories and workshops. One of the greatest boons working girls possess is a well-known eating-house in the City, where food is supplied at low prices. A plate of meat costs threepence, vegetables one penny, soup one half-penny, puddings three-halfpence. This eating-house was started by a member of the Y.W.C.A. some time ago, and is now almost self-supporting. The lady wanted to put the girls of her district into a club, but the doctor would not give them a certificate of health. He said, "Feed them first, and teach them the Gospel afterwards."

If more educated women would take up the

question of female labour, and work with as much charity and earnestness as Miss Black and the secretaries of the Y.W.C.A., we should soon have a different tale to tell about the work girls of London.

THE END.

Printed by Hazell, Watson, & Viney, Ld., London and Aylesbury.

www.ingramcontent.com/pod-product-compliance
Lightning Source LLC
Chambersburg PA
CBHW030352270326
41926CB00009B/1070

* 9 7 8 3 3 3 7 0 7 1 8 7 5 *